Humor in Healthcare:
The Laughter Prescription

WESTERN®
SCHOOLS

By
Enid A. Schwartz, RN, MS, MC

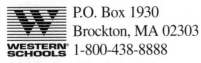

P.O. Box 1930
Brockton, MA 02303
1-800-438-8888

ABOUT THE AUTHOR

Enid A. Schwartz, RN, MS, MC is an instructor in nursing, behavioral health, and psychology. She taught nursing at Cochise College for 17 years, including a course on loss, grief, and dying, which she taught for 11 years on campus and 3 years online. She currently teaches nursing online and in the classroom for University of Phoenix. Ms. Schwartz has presented workshops for PESI HealthCare on humor in health-care, end-of-life issues and care of the dying, aging issues, and Alzheimer's disease. Along with two other nurses, Ms. Schwartz presents humor workshops as a member of the HaHa Sisterhood. She is also a certified laughter leader. She completed this certification with the World Laughter Tour in 2004. Her publications include "Your Jewish Patient is Dying," which appeared in the January/February 1989 issue of *AD Nurse* and a chapter about Jewish Americans in a transcultural nursing text: *Transcultural Nursing, Assessment and Intervention* by Giger and Davidhizar. Her clinical experience ranges from pediatrics to geriatrics. She received a diploma from Newton-Wellesley School of Nursing, a BSN and an MSN from the University of Arizona, and a Master's in Counseling from the University of Phoenix, Southeastern Arizona Campus. Ms. Schwartz is presently a PhD candidate at Walden University. Her dissertation focuses on using humor to cope with breast cancer.

Enid Schwartz has disclosed that she has no significant financial or other conflicts of interest pertaining to this course book.

ABOUT THE SUBJECT MATTER REVIEWER

Marion G. Anema, RN, PhD, is the faculty chair for the MS in Nursing Program, School of Health and Human Services, at Walden University. Her previous positions include dean of the School of Nursing at Tennessee State University in Nashville. She also teaches online courses on diversity, ethics, and professional nursing issues. She has written and published articles, continuing education courses, and online case studies and has been involved in the development of online nursing courses and programs for 10 years.

Marion Anema has disclosed that she has no significant financial or other conflicts of interest pertaining to this course book.

Nurse Planner: Amy Bernard, RN, BSN, MS
Copy Editors: Liz Schaeffer and Jaime Stockslager Buss
Indexer: Sylvia Coates

ISBN: 978-1-57801-131-5

IMPORTANT: Read these instructions *BEFORE* proceeding!

Enclosed with your course book, you will find the FasTrax® answer sheet. Use this form to answer all the final exam questions that appear in this course book. If you are completing more than one course, be sure to write your answers on the appropriate answer sheet. Full instructions and complete grading details are printed on the FasTrax instruction sheet, also enclosed with your order. Please review them before starting. *If you are mailing your answer sheet(s) to Western Schools, we recommend you make a copy as a backup.*

ABOUT THIS COURSE

A Pretest is provided with each course to test your current knowledge base regarding the subject matter contained within this course. Your Final Exam is a multiple choice examination. **You will find the exam questions at the end of each chapter.**

In the event the course has less than 100 questions, leave the remaining answer boxes on the FasTrax answer sheet blank. **Use a <u>black</u> pen to fill in your answer sheet.**

A PASSING SCORE

You must score 70% or better in order to pass this course and receive your Certificate of Completion. Should you fail to achieve the required score, we will send you an additional FasTrax answer sheet so that you may make a second attempt to pass the course. Western Schools will allow you three chances to pass the same course…*at no extra charge!* After three failed attempts to pass the same course, your file will be closed.

RECORDING YOUR HOURS

Please monitor the time it takes to complete this course using the handy log sheet on the other side of this page. See below for transferring study hours to the course evaluation.

COURSE EVALUATIONS

In this course book, you will find a short evaluation about the course you are soon to complete. This information is vital to providing Western Schools with feedback on this course. The course evaluation answer section is in the lower right hand corner of the FasTrax answer sheet marked "Evaluation," with answers marked 1–18. Your answers are important to us; please take a few minutes to complete the evaluation.

On the back of the FasTrax instruction sheet, there is additional space to make any comments about the course, the school, and suggested new curriculum. Please mail the FasTrax instruction sheet, with your comments, back to Western Schools in the envelope provided with your course order.

TRANSFERRING STUDY TIME

Upon completion of the course, transfer the total study time from your log sheet to question 18 in the course evaluation. The answers will be in ranges; please choose the proper hour range that best represents your study time. You **MUST** log your study time under question 18 on the course evaluation.

EXTENSIONS

You have two (2) years from the date of enrollment to complete this course. A six (6) month extension may be purchased. If after 30 months from the original enrollment date you do not complete the course, *your file will be closed and no certificate can be issued.*

CHANGE OF ADDRESS?

In the event you have moved during the completion of this course, please call our student services department at 1-800-618-1670, and we will update your file.

A GUARANTEE TO WHICH YOU'LL GIVE HIGH HONORS

If any continuing education course fails to meet your expectations or if you are not satisfied in any manner, for any reason, you may return it for an exchange or a refund (less shipping and handling) within 30 days. Software, video, and audio courses must be returned unopened.

Thank you for enrolling at Western Schools!

WESTERN SCHOOLS
P.O. Box 1930
Brockton, MA 02303
(800) 438-8888
www.westernschools.com

Humor in Healthcare:
The Laughter Prescription

WESTERN
SCHOOLS
P.O. Box 1930
Brockton, MA 02303

Please use this log to total the number of hours you spend reading the text and taking the final examination.

Date	Hours Spent
_____	_____
_____	_____
_____	_____
_____	_____
_____	_____
_____	_____
_____	_____
_____	_____
_____	_____
_____	_____
_____	_____
_____	_____
_____	_____

TOTAL _____

Please log your study hours with submission of your final exam. To log your study time, fill in the appropriate circle under question 18 of the FasTrax® answer sheet under the "Evaluation" section.

Humor in Healthcare:
The Laughter Prescription

WESTERN SCHOOLS
CONTINUING EDUCATION EVALUATION

Instructions: Mark your answers to the following questions with a black pen on the "Evaluation" section of your FasTrax® answer sheet provided with this course. You should not return this sheet.

Please use the scale below to rate how well the course content met the educational objectives.

A	**Agree Strongly**	**C**	**Disagree Somewhat**
B	**Agree Somewhat**	**D**	**Disagree Strongly**

After completing this course, I am able to

1. Discuss the meaning of humor and theories of humor.

2. Discuss the evolution of humor in healthcare as well as the history and development of humor in nursing.

3. Describe how humor can affect the immune system, physiological health, and pain management.

4. Discuss the psychosocial effects of humor.

5. Describe how humor develops from infancy to adulthood.

6. Explain how humor can be used in the healthcare setting to benefit nurses and their patients.

7. Analyze the appropriate use of humor in crises and disaster situations.

8. Discuss the effective use of humor in psychiatric settings.

9. Discuss the ways in which humor can be used in educational situations.

10. Discuss different types of formal humor programs and the concerns and considerations related to implementing a program.

11. Discuss ways to engage in humorous interchanges with patients, colleagues, and other healthcare providers.

12. The content of this course was relevant to the objectives.

13. This offering met my professional education needs.

14. The objectives met the overall purpose/goal of the course.

15. The course was generally well written and the subject matter was thoroughly explained . (If no, please explain on the back of the FasTrax instruction sheet.)

16. The content of this course was appropriate for home study.

17. The final examination was well written and at an appropriate level for the content of the course.

18. **PLEASE LOG YOUR STUDY HOURS WITH SUBMISSION OF YOUR FINAL EXAM.**
    Please choose the response that best represents the total study hours it took to complete this 20-hour course.

    A. Less than 15 hours   C. 19–21 hours

    B. 15–18 hours   D. Greater than 22 hours

CONTENTS

FIGURES AND TABLES

PRETEST

1. Begin this course by taking the pretest. Circle the answers to the questions on this page, or write the answers on a separate sheet of paper. Do not log answers to the pretest questions on the FasTrax test sheet included with the course.

2. Compare your answers to the PRETEST KEY located in the back of the book. The pretest answer key indicates the course chapter where the content of that question is discussed. Make note of the questions you missed, so that you can focus on those areas as you complete the course.

3. Complete the course by reading each chapter and completing the exam questions at the end of the chapter. Answers to these exam questions should be logged on the FasTrax test sheet included with the course.

1. One important aspect of the definition of humor is that
   a. everyone experiences humor the same way.
   b. humor is individualized.
   c. all humor leads to laughter.
   d. humor is simple to define.

2. An important distinction between humor and laughter is that humor is a cognitive function, whereas laughter is
   a. a release of energy.
   b. a fun experience.
   c. the only response to humor.
   d. a physiological response.

3. Florence Nightingale claimed that nurses needed to be sober, trustworthy, honest, chaste, and clean in order to
   a. prevent being labeled as impure and unclean.
   b. appear professional.
   c. prevent the use of indecent humor in their presence.
   d. obtain the money needed for cleaning up the wards.

4. The positive effects of humor have been known since
   a. biblical times.
   b. the 13th century.
   c. 1560.
   d. Plato's time.

5. Using humor as an adjunct to pain therapy
   a. increases the need for pain medication.
   b. decreases endorphin levels.
   c. decreases cytokine levels.
   d. increases the pain threshold.

6. Laughter helps improve
   a. muscle mass.
   b. weight loss.
   c. dancing ability.
   d. respiratory function.

7. Humor helps to diffuse anger by
   a. bringing people closer together.
   b. releasing pent-up emotions.
   c. increasing awareness to absurdity.
   d. dissolving barriers.

8. Humor works as an effective stress reducer because it

   a. releases endorphins.

   b. suppresses anger.

   c. increases denial.

   d. change a person's perspective.

9. An example of antisocial humor includes

   a. knock-knock jokes.

   b. cultural jokes.

   c. crazy antics.

   d. mispronounced or misused words.

10. Children laugh

    a. more than adults.

    b. at everything.

    c. rarely.

    d. only with other children.

11. Release of tension leads to

    a. frustration.

    b. decreased productivity.

    c. increased creativity.

    d. poor problem solving.

12. Nurses need to be careful not to initiate humor with patients

    a. when providing hands-on care.

    b. during the admission procedure.

    c. when the patient is experiencing a stressful event.

    d. when the patient is communicating about a nonstressful situation.

13. The use of humor assists victims after a crisis by

    a. allowing the merging of self with the crisis.

    b. decreasing defenses and coping mechanisms.

    c. restricting the survivors' perspectives.

    d. giving perspective on the crisis.

14. Humor offers prisoners of war a sense of

    a. hope.

    b. frustration.

    c. sorrow.

    d. joy.

15. In the therapeutic environment, humor is

    a. one way to express caring.

    b. used to mask hostility.

    c. destructive.

    d. anxiety provoking.

16. When used psychotherapeutically, humor can offer the patient

    a. a way of hiding.

    b. insight.

    c. false hope.

    d. relief.

17. One reason to add humor to the educational process is

    a. laughter is needed to make the material interesting.

    b. humor always aids the learning process.

    c. humor helps to increase motivation.

    d. students like teachers who use humor.

18. Adding humor to the lives of coworkers is
    as important as sharing humor with patients.
    One way of doing this appropriately is to

    a. pull practical jokes on each other.

    b. place cartoons on the bulletin board.

    c. keep a humor diary.

    d. watch sitcoms during work.

19. The most important element of sharing humor
    with others is

    a. watching funny movies.

    b. finding the humor within yourself.

    c. thinking of funny everyday situations.

    d. remembering an embarrassing story.

20. One way a person can increase humor
    awareness is to

    a. keep a humor diary.

    b. participate in a humor study.

    c. watch dramatic movies.

    d. read the personal ads.

INTRODUCTION

This continuing education program examines the holistic effects of humor on the health of individuals. It looks at the difference between humor and laughter, the development of humor studies, and the ways in which humor effects the biological, psychological, and sociological health of individuals. It also discusses ways nurses can incorporate humor into the care of individuals and their families. The target population for this workbook is any nurse who works with patients or wants to improve his or her knowledge about therapeutic humor.

The positive effects of humor have been known since biblical times. In the thirteenth century a physician became aware that laughter was helpful in recovery from surgery (Haig, 1988). In the mid 1500's observations led to the hypothesis that laughter contributed to the a healthy mind and body (Haig, 1988). Within the last 30 years, research on the physiological and psychological effects of humor has increased. Most of this research indicates that humor has a positive influence on the mind and body.

Klein (1989) states that "humor gives us power and a new perspective" (p. 3). Studies indicate that it helps us cope with stressful life events, provides strength to get through difficult situations, and offers a different viewpoint on situations (Klein, 1989; Kuiper, Martin, & Olinger, 1993; Lefcourt & Martin, 1986; Nezu, Nezu, & Blissett, 1988; Wiklinski, 1994). Being a patient is commonly stressful, and nurses must deal with this stress whenever they come in contact with patients. Understanding how humor can decrease tension, improve a person's perspective of a stressful situation, and help people cope with life events encourages nurses to add humor to their interventions.

One area of humor research that has received a lot of attention is the effect of humor on the immune system. The following effects have been documented: increases in natural killer cell activity, T-cell activity, and the production of immunoglobulins and some leukocytes. (Berk, Felten, Tan, Bittman, & Westengard, 2001). Decreases in the body's production of cortisol after viewing humor films have also been reported (Martin, 2001). Increased cortisol levels decrease the body's immune capabilities. Therefore, the use of humor may increase an individual's protection against certain diseases.

Humor has also been proven helpful in managing pain. Some of the information on humor and pain management comes from stories shared by those who have employed humor to help with their own pain, such as Norman Cousins' (1979) recounting of his experience in his book *Anatomy of an Illness as Perceived by the Patient*. In addition, several studies indicate a positive correlation between humor and pain management (Mahony, Burroughs, & Hieatt, 2001; Martin, 2001). Because humor seems to have a positive effect on pain management, nurses need to be aware of how this relationship works and what they can do to help patients use humor as an adjunct to pain medication.

Because research shows that humor has positive effects, it is important for nurses to take humor seriously. With that in mind, this book was designed to help nurses understand why and how to incorporate humor into the care of patients. The following chapters examine the history of humor in healthcare; its psychological, physiological, and sociologic effects; the development of humor throughout the life span; and ways to incorporate humor into our own lives and into the lives of others.

CHAPTER 1

DEFINITIONS AND THEORIES OF HUMOR

CHAPTER OBJECTIVES

After completing this chapter, the reader will be able to discuss the meaning of humor and theories of humor.

LEARNING OBJECTIVES

After studying this chapter, the learner will be able to

1. define humor.
2. describe the differences between humor and laughter.
3. identify the properties that cause a humor response.
4. discuss different theories of humor.

DEFINITION OF HUMOR

The word *humor* has many definitions. It is a multifaceted response to a stimuli. In order to have some understanding of what humor is, it is important to examine how different individuals define it. During this discussion, remember that many disciplines have attempted to define and explain humor.

Philosophers, psychologists, psychoanalysts, anthropologists, sociologists, physiologists, dramatists, playwrights, poets, prose writers, satirists, comedians, and others have attempted to define humor (Robinson,

1991). Ziegler (1998) notes that humor may be looked at as "communication (written, verbal, drawn or otherwise displayed) including teasing, jokes, witticisms, satire, sarcasm, cartoon, puns, clowning which induces (or is intended to induce) amusement, with or without laughing or smiling" (p. 342). Shibles (2002) states that it is a "mistake (and also a joke) to think there is a single definition of humor" (chap. 3, ¶ 3).

The current word *humor* is derived from two words, the Latin word *umor* and the medieval word *humor,* meaning fluid. Both of these words were medical terms referring to a biological temperament or disposition (Bokun, 1986). One use of the term in this context is humoral theory, the classical theory of health and illness. The humoral theory was based on the four body fluids referred to as *humors*: black bile, yellow bile, phlegm, and blood. Each of these humors was associated with mood: yellow bile (or choler), anger; black bile, melancholy; phlegm, apathy; and blood, confidence (Seaward, 1992). Variations in temperaments and illness were believed to result when the humors were mixed in different quantities. The combination of these body fluids resulted in a person being in "good humor" or "bad humor" (Haig, 1988). Physiologically, humor can be viewed as fluid within the body, such as blood or lymph. Bottari (2000) noted, "What better way to help heal anyone than by getting his/her own body to react to the healing process of engaging the blood and the lymphatic system" (¶ 2).

According to *Webster's Dictionary* (1985), humor is "the quality that makes something seem funny, amusing, or ludicrous" (p. 646). Another definition is "the ability to perceive, appreciate, or express what is funny, amusing, or ludicrous" (p. 646). The former refers to the state of something being amusing or absurd. The other refers to an individual's ability to perceive and appreciate something as humorous.

Vera Robinson (1991), one of the first nurses to write about the use of humor in healthcare settings, defines humor as "any communication which is perceived by any of the interacting parties as humorous and leads to laughing, smiling, and (or) a feeling of amusement" (p. 10). Robinson (1991) also views humor as a "cognitive communication leading to an emotional response of amusement, pleasure and mirth, which results in a behavioral physical response of laughter and its counterparts" (p. 10).

Berger (1987) says humor is "not so much a subject as an attitude, a stance, a 'sense' of things that we adopt, that colors the way we function in the universe" (p. 14). Perhaps it is the way humor "colors the way we function" that enables people to use humor for coping with stressful situations.

Humor is a form of communication. Both *Merriam-Webster's* dictionary and Robinson's definitions refer to other's perceptions of the message that is given. Each of us may interpret a message differently. For example how many times have you been in a situation in which someone said something that was not meant to be funny but another person heard the message in such a way that it seemed funny to him or her? Or, how about a message that was meant to be funny but the receiver either did not understand the humor or was offended by what was said.

Shibles (2002) mentions that humor is an emotion. Emotions cause bodily feelings and actions. Humor results in feelings and actions in a certain context. In a different environment or emotional state of being, the same thing that caused a humor response in one case may cause a different reaction or level of reaction in a different context. Humor allows us to see ourselves and our situations from diverse, different, curious, and extraordinary perspectives.

The Association for Applied and Therapeutic Humor defines *therapeutic humor* as "any intervention that promotes health and wellness by stimulating a playful discovery, expression or appreciation of the absurdity or incongruity of life's situations. This intervention may enhance health or be used as a complementary treatment of illness to facilitate healing or coping whether physical, emotional, cognitive, social or spiritual" (Humor Matters, n.d., ¶ 1).

The humanistic psychologist Rollo May defined humor as a healthy way of feeling a "distance" between oneself and the problem, a way of standing off and looking at one's problem with perspective (Humor Matters, n.d.). James Thurber stated that "humor is emotional chaos remembered in tranquility" (Humor Matters, n.d., p.1).

Looking at the different definitions of humor, it is apparent that everyone has a belief about what humor is. This is one reason why researching humor is difficult. We can measure laughter and the effect it has, but how do we quantify humor? As this text will demonstrate, however humor is defined, it is an important element in our daily functioning and in maintaining our emotional and physical health.

THE DIFFERENCES BETWEEN LAUGHTER AND HUMOR

Most definitions of humor include the element of laughter. However, humor and laughter do not always go hand in hand. It is actually a misconception that *laughter* and *humor* can be used interchangeably. Humor and laughter are qualitatively different (Mahony, 2000). Humor is a cognitive response to a stimulus, whereas laughter is a physiological response. Solomon (1996) explains the cognitive process of humor in three steps, beginning with arousal, followed by problem solving, and finally understanding the resolution, or "getting the joke."

Not everything a person finds humorous results in the behavior we call *laughter*. Responses to humor may include a twinkling of the eyes, a giggle, a feeling of lightness within, a change in facial expression, or even a groan. One participant in an unpublished humor study by Schwartz (personal communication, March, 1999) stated that "humor allows the spirit to be free." Laughter may be a response to tickling, surprise, embarrassment, tension, relief after tension, or play.

As previously mentioned, humor is the perception of something being funny. Laughter is the physiological response to humor. The psychophysiological aspects of humor have been partitioned into three elements: 1) the stimulus (humor); 2) the emotional response (a feeling of mirth); and 3) the physical response (laughter).

In addition to laughter, other behavioral responses can occur in response to humor. These responses include smirking, smiling, grinning, giggling, and chuckling. When something is perceived as very funny, a person may start laughing and the laughter can become increasingly physical.

The trigger of laughter could be a humorous stimuli or the sound of shared laughter. For example, Annette Goodheart, a humor therapist, comes to workshops with her bear, Charlie. She walks out on stage and starts to giggle. Then the giggle turns into laughter. In the audience, one can hear giggles as Goodheart starts her giggling. As Goodheart continues, almost everyone in the audience begins to giggle and laugh. Eventually, for just about every member of the audience, it is hard not to laugh. Goodheart's approach demonstrates that laughter is infectious and the humor stimulus could be the sound of another's laughter rather than a joke or funny incident.

What is it about laughter that makes it contagious? Provine (2000a), who has studied laughter as a behavior, theorizes that the contagious response of humans to laughter suggests that individuals might have some type of neurological trigger that results in the movement of the thorax, larynx, and vocal chords that creates the sound of laughter. He refers to this neurological trigger as the "laugh-dector." This laugh-dector somehow activates the laugh-generator.

HUMOR THEORIES

Humor is multifaceted. It is the lack of universally accepted definition that makes the study of humor and its affects complicated. The theories that arise because of these multifaceted aspects cover the nature of humor or the purpose of humor. Other theories describe the nature of laughter. Sometimes humor and laughter are used interchangeably. However, as previously noted, the two are not synonymous.

What makes things appear funny or humorous? Multiple theories have been developed to attempt to explain the phenomenon (Haig, 1988; Wilson, 1979), yet the concept remains difficult to define. Wilson (1979) notes that humor, which is everywhere, seems to defy examination. Scholars have been trying to define the essence of humor since the era of Plato and Aristotle (Haig, 1988; Holland, 1982; Wilson, 1979). This attempt continues today.

Haig (1988) examined more than 100 theories about humor and organized them into five theoretical categories: tension-release theories, theories of superiority, theories of social communication, psychoanalytic theories, and incongruity theories. Berger (1987) claims there are three important theories of humor: superiority theory, psychoanalytic theory, and cognitive theory. Harvey (1998) discusses play theory, which is based on a belief that play is an important part of humor. However, according to Holland (1982), none of these theories have reached general acceptance. Table 1-1 provides a summary of humor theories.

TABLE 1-1: OVERVIEW OF HUMOR THEORIES	
Superiority	Laughing at those who make mistakes
Psychoanalytic	A socially accepted way of suppressing unaccepted behavior, such as with sexual jokes
Incongruity	Results of the joke or experience are incongruent
Cognitive	The brain's processing of information that leads to a resolution that produces a sense of amusement
Play	Playfulness that allows the person to see the humorous parts of life or cause laughter in others

Superiority Theory

According to the Greek philosophers, Plato and Aristotle, comedy was a way of imitating the worst of man. Some philosophers saw laughter as a weapon to use against evil and a way to help correct the absurdities of society. Using this type of humor presumably gives pleasure from feelings of superiority when we observe those of lower status and contrast their ways with ours. Whisonant (1998) notes that this theory has fallen out of favor in the last couple of decades. Although it is true that humor can be used as a way to depict the negative in man, this attitude may have hampered the study of humor and the development of humor theories.

This superiority aspect of humor is exemplified by the pleasure that a person takes when someone makes a mistake. The story about the new student nurse who is sent to the supply room by another nurse to get a fallopian tube is an example of humor that leads to feelings of superiority over those who make mistakes.

Superiority can also be seen in situations in which laughter conveys warmth and empathy. This is based on the recognition that the situation did not

happen to us, but it could. This aspect of humor can be described as being on a continuum, from laughing at no one, to laughing at someone or others, to laughing with others at man's general failings, to laughing at oneself. Robinson (1991) notes that laughing at oneself "may be the key ingredient in the coping, survival function of humor and laughter" (p. 20).

Psychoanalytic Theory

In his 1960 book *Jokes and Their Relation to the Unconscious,* Freud stated that jokes are a socially acceptable way of satisfying man's need to repress impulses that are not viewed as socially acceptable. He theorized that humor gives pleasure by permitting brief gratification of some hidden or forbidden wish, at the same time reducing the anxiety occurring from the inhibition of the wish. Freud saw humor as a way for adults to think like children and escape the constraints of rationality and logic. This theory defines humor as a socially acceptable way of releasing built-up tension and nervous energy. This theory is also referred to as *relief theory*.

Freud differentiated between what he considered "innocent" and "tendentious" jokes. Tendentious jokes are those that have sexual or aggressive content and the ability to elicit howling laughter. Innocent jokes have less emotional impact and tend to cause a chuckle or less. Sexual humor allows us to disguise sexual aggression and hostility (Berger, 1987).

Strubbe (2003) mentions that the laughter of relief may have been our ancestors' way of signaling the passing of a life-and-death threat. This relief response is commonly used in the film industry, when tension and suspense build to a crescendo and then an aside or sight gag is interjected to allow a release. In life, relief laughter can allow a person to cope with stressful or dangerous situations.

Relief humor may be experienced in response to "dirty jokes" because these jokes attempt to deal with the tension of sexual inhibitions. For example, during the funeral preparations for the author's husband's funeral, she asked the rabbis officiating to add a little humor because humor was something important to her husband. Her husband, Joe, loved to talk. At the funeral, one of the rabbis shared his first meeting with Joe. He shared how he took him on a tour of the area and stated, "And he talked, and he talked, and he talked." Giggles could be heard throughout the funeral home because those who knew Joe well could identify with how he talked.

Incongruity Theory

Many theorists claim that incongruity is the main ingredient of humor. According to Leise (1993), this includes "the ability to perceive absurdity in serious situations" (¶ 2). Incongruity theory seems to be the most widely accepted theory. This theory encompasses the element of surprise that comes with the conflict of ideas or emotions that results in a burst of laughter. "The punch lines generates a surprise, and an incongruous situation leads to laughter or some kind of humorous response" (Berger, 1987, p. 8). An example of this theory is seen in fractured communication or the misuse of words. For example, a volunteer entered a patient's room wearing oversized plastic eyeglasses with prescription pill bottles taped on each side of the frames. A young patient said, "I like your glasses." "They're her prescription glasses," deadpanned one of the nurses. The following charting examples also illustrate incongruity theory:

- "Discharge status: Alive, but without permission."

- "Patient ate whole tray."

- "By the time she was admitted to the hospital, her rapid heart had stopped, and she was feeling much better."

- "Patient referred to hospital by private physician with green stools."

- "Mycostatin vaginal suppositories. Insert daily until exhausted."

Another example of humor that fits within the incongruity theory is seen in a W.C. Fields joke. Someone asked Mr. Fields, "Do you believe in clubs for young people?" Fields replied, "Only when kindness fails."

Cognitive Theory

Cognitive theory is concerned with the way the brain processes information and focuses on the information we categorize as humor (Berger, 1987). From the cognitive perspective, "humor involves a resolution of logical paradoxes and other logical problems" (Berger, 1987, p. 10). Berger refers to this theory as semiotic, or the science of signs. He contends that a comic film, for example, is a series of signs and codes that people interpret to make meaning. How people process this interpretation (cognitive work) is the focus of semiotic analysis that can lead to the response known as humor.

Interpretation of a Joke by Four Theorists

Berger (1987) analyzed a joke from the perspective of the four theories mentioned above. Let's look at this analysis as a way of understanding how humans can process jokes, with the resulting behavioral response of laughter or at least the emotion of mirth. For his analysis, Berger chose the following joke as an example:

A man goes to Miami for a vacation. After 5 days there, he looks in the mirror and notices he has a gorgeous tan all over his body, except where his thong swim suit covered him. He decides to remedy the situation. The next morning he gets up early, goes to a deserted section of the beach, and starts putting sand all over his body until only his untanned body part is exposed above the sand. Two little old ladies happen to walk by just as he has finished shoveling the sand all over himself. One of the ladies notices him and tells her friend "When I was 20, I was scared to death of them," she says. "When I was 40, I couldn't get enough of them," she continues. "When I was 60, I couldn't get one to come near me. And now they're growing wild on the beach."

A superiority theorist would say that we laugh because we feel superior to the characters in the story. The man is seen as foolish for thinking he must have a tan at any expense. The woman, who thinks that private parts can grow wild on the beach, demonstrates ignorance.

Freud would have a good time with this joke. From his psychoanalytic viewpoint, the humor response from this joke comes from its sexual content. In this case, humor is related to sexuality and, particularly, sexual hunger as it changes with age. The joke not only has a woman who thinks private body parts can grow wild on the beach but also has a man who demonstrates exhibitionist tendencies.

An incongruity theorist would explain that the humor comes from the absurdity that a person would only have that body part sticking out of the sand or that this body part might grow wild on the beach. The punch line is the incongruent part of the joke. In addition, there is something bizarre about someone burying his body and leaving his private parts open to potential public view. Most of the joke sets up the story, or develops the framework. The last line seems incongruent, which leads to laughter.

From the perspective of a cognitive theorist, the joke has a "play frame" that is established by the man's bizarre behavior and desire to tan every part of his body. According to Berger (1987), "this play frame allows us to view the crazy notion of the woman that penises might grow wild on the beach as funny and not to be taken seriously" (p. 11-12).

Play Theory

Another theory holds that play is an essential part of humor (Harvey, 1998). Play theory purports that "the enjoyment of something laughable comes from the arousal of a playful mood" (Harvey, 1998, p. 43). McGhee (1994) believes that playfulness is

an important element in seeing the humorous parts of life. He states that playfulness is "the basic foundation for your sense of humor" (p. 56). McGhee (1994) also states that playfulness leads to increased spontaneity and enjoyment, which allows the mind to process experiences as more humorous than it can when you are serious. If this is true, then adding a sense of playfulness into nursing can result in more enjoyment of the professional aspects of nursing and improved relationships between all individuals with whom the nurse comes in contact.

Have you ever walked into a room and experienced a sense of tension that felt very uncomfortable? Maybe someone just had a fight with someone else, or maybe someone is dying or in a lot of pain. Whatever the problem, the room felt full of negative vibes. If a measure of playfulness, done with sensitivity and respect, was brought into this environment, theoretically it could help lighten the mood. Take the following situation as an example: A doctor's patient is very ill and the doctor does not want to leave the patient for long. He misses his dinner. He is sitting with the patient when the nurse walks in to see if there is anything she can do. The doctor complains of being hungry and asks her to bring him something. Dietary service is closed, and there is nothing on the unit except custard and juice. The doctor desires something more substantial, but none of the units have anything more to offer. The doctor, probably due to hunger, becomes more irritable. The nurse remembers that the humor cart has a rubber chicken. She gets the chicken, puts a blue ribbon around its neck, folds it into a dish, puts a silver cover over it, and brings it to the doctor. His eyes light up when he sees the dish; he takes the cover off and the chicken unfolds. In anger, he says, "What the hell is this?" The nurse looks and says, "I think it is Chicken Cord n' Blue." At that, the doctor starts to laugh, and the nurse and doctor laugh together. She then brings him the custard and juice, which he finishes joyfully.

SUMMARY

Humor defies a specific definition. It is a response to stimuli that causes positive changes. The change may be one of mood, attitude, hope, or perhaps a connection to others. The response to humor is sometimes laughter, but laughter and humor are not the same. Humor is a perception; laughter is a behavioral response.

As there are multiple definitions of humor, there are also multiple theories of humor. The most popular one among researchers is incongruity theory. Whatever theory one believes, we know that humor has physical and psychosocial value.

EXAM QUESTIONS

CHAPTER 1
Questions 1-9

1. Laughter is best defined as

    a. an indicator that humor is effective.

    b. the same as humor.

    c. a learned response to humor.

    d. a behavioral response to humor.

2. Humor consists of

    a. communication, feelings of amusement, and multifaceted parts.

    b. communication, a specific definition, and feelings of amusement.

    c. communication, mood alteration ability, and negative physical stimuli.

    d. feelings of amusement, mood alteration ability, and exaggerated response.

3. The most important component of humor is

    a. its ability to cause feelings of amusement.

    b. its mood-altering effect that simulates morphine's effects.

    c. its ability to produce a negative immunological effect.

    d. the sense of superiority it reflects.

4. The psychophysiological response to humor has been divided into three main elements. These elements are

    a. stimulus, perception, and emotional response.

    b. stimulus, emotional response, and physical response.

    c. emotional response, cognitive response, and physical response.

    d. emotional response, receiver of the message, and physical response.

5. The difference between humor and laughter is

    a. humor is a perception, and laughter is a feeling.

    b. humor causes a feeling of lightness, and laughter causes feelings of tension.

    c. humor is a perception, and laughter is a physiological response.

    d. humor causes feelings of mirth, and laughter is the cause of humor.

6. According to Freud, a tendentious joke would elicit a

    a. giggle.

    b. smile.

    c. smirk.

    d. howl.

7. A student nurse was taking care of a patient
    who was on bed rest with commode privileges.
    When the patient asked to go to the bathroom,
    the student put the commode on the bed for
    the patient to use. A nursing instructor
    started to laugh when she heard this story. This
    form of humor would most likely fall under
    the humor theory of

    a. superiority.

    b. social communication.

    c. psychoanalytic.

    d. tension release.

8. The element of humor that occurs in reading
    nurses' notes that contain misused words falls
    under the theory of

    a. tension release.

    b. superiority theory.

    c. incongruity theory.

    d. social communication.

9. The most popular theory of humor is the

    a. psychoanalytic theory.

    b. cognitive theory.

    c. superiority theory.

    d. incongruity theory.

CHAPTER 2

THE HISTORY OF HUMOR IN NURSING

CHAPTER OBJECTIVE

After completing this chapter, the reader will be able to discuss the evolution of humor in nursing as well as the history and development of humor in nursing.

LEARNING OBJECTIVES

After studying this chapter, the reader will be able to

1. discuss the history of humor in nursing.

2. describe how the use of humor in nursing has changed through the years.

3. discuss the early recognition of the importance of humor in health maintenance.

4. identify contributing elements to the interest in humor research.

THE HISTORY OF HUMOR IN NURSING

Humor has been used in nursing since at least the time of Florence Nightingale. From accounts presented in notes on the Crimean War and letters written by Nightingale, it is apparent that humor was one way Nightingale dealt with the horrors, filth, and stresses of war. For example, in 1858, Nightingale wrote a letter to the Secretary of War from Scutari, Crimea, describing the filth. She stat-

ed, "The vermin might, if they had but unity of purpose, carry off the four miles of beds on their backs and march them into the War Office" (Kelly, 1981, p. 30).

In her "Duties of Probationer" for the first Training School for Nurses in 1860, Nightingale required nurses to be patient, cheerful, and kindly (Kelly, 1981). She appears to have set the tone for restrained use of humor by reminding students to be sober, trustworthy, honest, chaste, and clean in order to prevent a situation in which an "immodest jest" would be spoken in a nurse's presence.

Looking back over the years, it is apparent that the type of humor in and about nursing has changed. Of course, that is also true about humor in general. There is little, if any, record of the use of humor between patient and nurse before the 1960s. That does not mean that humor was not used, but rather that the deliberate use of humor for communication, teaching, or therapeutic intervention was not documented before that time. The humor that can be found before 1960 tends to reflect patients' perceptions about nurses and the care they received (Robinson, 1991). Robinson (1991) notes that this humor tends to reflect four stereotypical images of nurses: the servant or handmaiden, the nurturer, the sex-object, and the old battle-axe. These perceptions of nurses most likely resulted from patients' fears, anxieties, and misconceptions.

Humor about nurses has changed as nursing has become a more respected profession. Nurses are not depicted in negative stereotypes or as sexual objects as often as they were in previous years. As nursing evolved, the ability of nurses to laugh at themselves grew. The first cartoons about nurses for nurses appeared in *RN* magazine in the early 1940s. For the first 6 months of nursing training, a student was considered a probationer, or "Probie." Many of the cartoons of this era made fun of the "Probie." The cartoons that appeared in *RN* commonly involved dumb student incidents, practical jokes, and gallows humor. This type of humor was often vividly remembered and was therapeutic for the nurse.

The use of patient-related humor is less obvious because it was not encouraged in the 1940s. Such humor did exist, however. There were jokes about hospital gowns that did not cover enough and flapped in the breeze, hospital food, bedpans, and "finishing the bath!" (Robinson, 1991). Jokes about these types of situations were the main types of humor up until the 1960s.

In the 1950s and 1960s, cartoons appeared in *RN*, the *American Journal of Nursing* (*AJN*), and *Medical Economics*. In 1976, Thelma Canarecci compiled her cartoons in *Odds & Ends of Ward Wit*. *AJN* also printed a "time off" page, which presented information that offered some lighter, sometimes funny or nostalgic material.

Robinson (1991) notes that during the 1960s, "with the advent of community mental health, psychosocial nursing, recognizing and meeting the emotional needs of patients, moving to a focus on health promotion rather than disease, and a humanistic approach to nursing, that we first began to take humor seriously" (p. 11). Articles that looked at humorous topics or discussed issues regarding the use of humor with patients began appearing in nursing magazines. Humor started to become accepted as a therapeutic tool.

In 1965, Vera Robinson began to research how nurses used humor. She explored the history of humor in healthcare, particularly between nurses and patients. The research began as a grant from the National Institute of Mental Health (NIMH). She later expanded on this research for her doctoral dissertation. The first school she attended attempted to dissuade her from doing her dissertation on humor because it was not considered a professional subject. She subsequently changed universities so that she could continue to pursue her interest in humor and healthcare. Today, numerous dissertations on humor in nursing are available. These studies cover such issues as the use of humor by cancer patients (Wiklinski, 1994); humor communication between nurses and residents in a long-term care residence (Lippert, 2001); and the use of humor as a coping mechanism in prisoners of war (Henman, 2001).

Vera Robinson was also the first nurse to publish a text on *Humor and the Health Professions*. This text, published in 1978, resulted from the work she had done on her dissertation. Her book covers many aspects of humor and health, including the value of humor in health, the use of humor by nurses when interacting with patients, and ways to bring more humor into healthcare settings. At the time Robinson started her dissertation, using humor was seen as unprofessional. In just 15 years, humor had become a scholarly subject that was considered acceptable to research and teach. In the 1980s, nurses began incorporating humor into education, practice, and management (Robinson, 1991).

In 1988, a nurse named Alison Crane started the American Association for Therapeutic Humor (AATH) to advance the dissemination of humor in healthcare. By 2000, the organization had grown and the name was changed to the Association for Applied and Therapeutic Humor to reflect the direction the association had taken. A number of AATH members are nurses who are well known in the therapeutic humor community, such as Patty Wooten, Karen Buxman, Leslie Gibson, and Mark Darby. Each of these people have worked to further advance the knowledge of the benefits of therapeutic humor.

A Nursing Humor Journal is Born

Until a tragic accident took his life in 1997, Doug Fletcher was the publisher of the *Journal of Nursing Jocularity* (*JNJ*). The first issue of *JNJ* was published in Spring of 1991. The magazine was published quarterly for nurses and other health professionals and was written, illustrated, edited, and published completely by nurses and other health professionals. The magazine took risks by presenting humor that was sometimes macabre. However, as Fletcher (1991) stated in one of his editorials, "The closer our work is to pain and death, the darker our humor is. [Emergency room] and [intensive care unit] nurses are some of the sickest nurses I know when it comes to humor" (p. 128). The magazine included articles about the therapeutic use of humor; reviews of current books, tapes, and toys related to humor and healthcare; jokes; satire; stories; and interviews with experts in the area of psychoneuroimmunology. In its seventh year of publication, *JNJ* had more than 35,000 subscribers from all 50 states and Canada (Wooten, 1997).

JNJ reflected the humor of the present-day nurse. There were jokes and stories about managed care. There were jokes about situations in emergency rooms, intensive care units, and other areas. Some of the humor was dark humor that encouraged laughing about death and disfigurement. This type of humor is sometimes referred to as "gallows" humor because it revolves around someone who is facing disgusting or heartbreaking situations. All humor serves a purpose: to help relieve stress and to make the present situation bearable and lighter. In many cases, the grimmer the situation, the darker the humor becomes.

Along with the magazine, *JNJ* sponsored a humor and health workshop every summer from 1991 until Fletcher's death. The workshops were designed to present information about the use of therapeutic humor in healthcare, and they contained valuable information about the use of humor. The workshops also served as a means for nurses to rec-ognize the effectiveness of humor as a stress-reduction technique because most of the presentations were designed to elicit laughter.

Prior to his death, Fletcher and several other nurses developed a program called *Who's Got the Keys?* This song-and-dance show was a spoof on nursing, its history, and the effects of managed care on nursing and patient care. A video of the show was made and this author has used the video as a humorous and effective means of educating student nurses.

The Development of Laughter Clubs

In 1998, Steve Wilson, a psychologist who also refers to himself as a "joyologist," had the opportunity to go to India, where he met Dr. Mandan Kataria, the founder and president of Laughter Club International. Wilson, who has studied humor and health, felt there was great potential for adding joy to people's lives by teaching them a systemic routine for laughing without using jokes. Dr. Kataria calls this exercise "laughter yoga." With support from his wife and the assistance of Karyn Buxman, a nurse and professional speaker on humor and health, Wilson developed World Laughter Tour (WLT). The slogan for WLT is "Think Globally, Laugh Locally." Since its inception, "WLT has come to be recognized as a significant global influence in the practical applications of laughter and humor for health and world peace" (WLT, n.d., ¶3).

The WLT offers training classes for those interested in becoming a Certified Laughter Leader (CLL). The classes are two days of education and laughter. The information covered includes the science of laughter, plus the theory, philosophy and physical aspects of the laughter exercises that are taught. After the training experience, Laughter Leaders are encouraged to start Laughter Clubs. Laughter Clubs exist in various locations, including nursing homes, assisted living facilities, elementary schools, communities, libraries, and colleges. Many CLL's are nurses, but there are also social workers, psychologists, counselors, health care staff workers, and even those who work in construction. Anyone interested in teaching others the benefits of laughter by conducting Laughter Clubs are encouraged to participate in the training classes.

Among the published goals of WLT are:

☺ To bring people of various countries together and promote events that bring everlasting peace through laughter

☺ To create a membership-based organization for the support of WLT as a self-sustaining organization

☺ To disseminate accredited training around the world and to develop models for advanced training using traditional educational methods as well as modern technological innovations, such as distance learning

☺ To develop a cadre of competent, accredited trainers who can train and certify Laughter Leaders

☺ To promote the adoption of Laughter Clubs in public places that can be free and open to everyone

☺ To promote the adoption of Laughter Clubs in every long-term care facility in the United States, as well as in schools, government offices, and workplaces, as an effective, reputable, professional program, on a fee-for-service basis wherever it is appropriate

☺ To create a professional association for accredited Laughter Leaders and providers of therapeutic laughter programs to enhance credibility and spread the access to these methods around the world

☺ To foster international conferences, meetings, and symposia on the therapeutic benefits of laughter and laughter methods to foster research and the sharing of research findings

(WLT, n.d.)

THE GROWTH OF HUMOR RESEARCH

Knowledge of the benefits of humor has been around for centuries. For example, the Bible states in Proverbs 17:22, "A merry heart doeth good like a medicine." Haig (1988) writes that Henri de Mondeville, a 13th century physician, believed that laughter assisted in recovery from surgery. During the 16th century, Martin Luther employed humor in his pastoral counseling of depressed people (Wells, 2001). He suggested that they surround themselves with friends who could joke and make them laugh rather than isolate themselves. In 1560, a prominent physician in Renaissance France, Laurent Joubert, hypothesized that being joyful and ready to laugh contributed to the health of the mind and the body. He formed this hypothesis after watching three ill people become healthy after laughing at the antics of monkeys (Haig, 1988).

In the 1860s, the scientist Herbert Spencer noted that laughter had a tension-relieving effect (Haig, 1988). The psychologist, William McDougall stated in 1903, that laughter stimulated the respiratory and cardiac systems, causing a euphoria that broke up the thoughts of pain and sadness (Haig, 1988). This theory has been substantiated to some extent in various studies (Leise, 1993). In 1923, McDougall made known his belief that humor served as a survival mechanism because it is nature's antidote to depressing and sad events experienced by humans (Leise, 1993).

According to Strubbe (2003), the scientific study of laughter has contributed an expanding body of research. The field is referred to as gelotology, from the Greek *gelos*, meaning "laughter." The first humor research studies occurred in the 1930s (Gibson, 1995). These studies found that the initial effect of laughter is stimulatory. Pulse and respiratory rates increase with laughter and, after laughter subsides, there is a brief relaxation phase.

The study of humor and health had its true beginnings in the 1960s, with the research of Dr. William Fry. Dr. Fry, a psychiatrist and professor emeritus from Standford Medical School, became interested in humor research through his study of paralinguistics. Paralinguistics involves nonverbal communication forms, such as sobbing and laughing. Fry was also curious about the physiological responses to humor. Using a pulse oximeter, he investigated the change in oxygen saturation after 3 minutes of continuous laughter. He found there was no change. However, he did find that laughter resulted in increased ventilation, increased muscle activity, increased minute volume, and the creation of forceful exhalation that could mobilize secretions.

In 1976, Norman Cousins wrote an article for the *New England Journal of Medicine* about his experience using humor in dealing with ankylosing spondylitis, a painful and progressive rheumatoid disease that causes inflammation of all joints, particularly the intervertebral disks of the spine. In 1979, Cousins expanded this article into his famous book, *Anatomy of an Illness as Perceived by the Patient*. In this book, Cousins shared how 10 minutes of hearty laughter provided 2 hours of pain-free sleep. The discussion of the effects of humor by Cousins was anecdotal, but it triggered interest in the use of humor as a pain-management strategy. From the experience of this nonmedical person, the study of humor and health really started to grow.

In 1986, Lefcourt and Martin proposed that humor might be a moderator of life stress (Haig, 1988). They produced evidence demonstrating that humor had a moderating effect on mood in normal college students who were experiencing increasing numbers of negative life events. They developed two questionnaires, the Situational Humor Response Questionnaire (SHRQ) and the Coping and Humor Scale (CHS), both of which are still used in many of the quantitative studies conducted on humor today.

PSYCHO-NEUROIMMUNOLOGY

Before the 1960s, common belief was that the mind and the body were separate entities. However, research examining mind-body interactions has shown that our mental state has a significant effect on our physical health and well-being. Specifically, studies indicate a connection between emotional status and the immune and neuroendocrine system.

The field of psychoneuroimmunology (PNI) began in the 1970s. At that time, this new field of study was considered controversial. However, substantial evidence now supports the belief that the mind and body communicate with one another through a bidirectional flow of hormones, cytokines, and neuropeptides (Watkins, 1997). The increased scientific evidence about the mind-body relationship clearly demonstrates that mood, thoughts, emotions, and belief systems can have an impact on the body's basic healing and health mechanisms (McGhee, 2000).

Studies examining PNI and the influence of humor have focused on the hypothalamus-pituitary-adrenal (HPA) axis and the sympathetic nervous system (Berk, Felten, Tan, Bittman, & Westengard, 2001). Berk and colleagues (2001) refer to the type of stress that is modulated by humor as a eustress experience. Eustress is a positive emotional state. The humor studies these researchers conducted looked at the effect of eustress induced by mirthful laughter on cortisol and catecholamines, which are products of both the HPA axis and the sympathetic nervous system. Additionally, Berk and colleagues (2001) have investigated laughter's effect on other hormones, such as growth hormones and prolactin, and the effect of humor on opioid peptides.

McGhee (2000) notes that some people believe that good coping skills help sustain health and well-being. Improving and taking advantage of a sense of humor is a fun way of coping with daily hassles.

Mia Smitt (1995), a hospice nurse, comments that "humor is a PNI therapy." She makes this claim based on evidence that humor is beneficial to health because it enhances the immune system. It is also a mediator of stress. The physiological effects of humor, including its effects on the immune system, will be explored in more detail in chapter 3.

SUMMARY

Humor's ability to affect our health has been recognized since biblical times. However, only relatively recently has humor become a subject of research. As society becomes more aware of the benefits of humor, humor has become accepted as an effective intervention for healthcare providers. Humor in nursing, and healthcare in general, has gone from being covert to overt. Laughter Clubs and hospital humor programs are examples of successful humor interventions.

EXAM QUESTIONS

CHAPTER 2
Questions 10-18

10. The first nursing cartoons appeared in *RN* magazine in the

    a. 1960s.
    b. 1950s.
    c. 1940s.
    d. 1930s.

11. The first nursing humor research was conducted by

    a. the NIMH.
    b. William Fry.
    c. Alison Crane.
    d. Vera Robinson.

12. Stereotypical depictions of nurses include the nurse as a servant or handmaiden, a nurturer, a sex-object, and

    a. a bearer of pain.
    b. an old battle-axe.
    c. an autonomous health provider.
    d. a scatterbrain.

13. A relatively recent global influence in promoting the practical application of humor for health and world peace is

    a. the development of the American Association for Therapeutic Humor (AATH).
    b. the development of the World Laughter Tour (WLT).
    c. research findings by Dr. William Fry.
    d. Norman Cousins' book *Anatomy of an Illness as Perceived by the Patient*.

14. The first written reference to the importance of happiness and health occurs in

    a. the Bible.
    b. the writings of Henri de Mondeville.
    c. the writings of Laurent Joubert.
    d. *The Saturday Evening Post*.

15. Dr. William Fry's interest in humor developed from his interest in

    a. pain management.
    b. psychology.
    c. verbal communication.
    d. non verbal communication.

16. In the 13th century, Henri de Mondeville observed that laughter appears to help

    a. control pain.
    b. recover from surgery.
    c. stimulate the immune system.
    d. reduce stress.

17. While dealing with the pain of ankylosing spondylitis, Norman Cousins found that 10 minutes of hearty laughter left him pain free for

    a. 2 hours.
    b. 2.5 hours.
    c. 3 hours.
    d. 3.5 hours.

18. Recent studies show that communication between the mind and body occurs through

    a. conscious thought and concentration.

    b. hormones, cytokines, and neuropeptides.

    c. the gastroenterology system.

    d. the parasympathetic nervous system.

CHAPTER 3

THE PHYSIOLOGICAL EFFECTS OF HUMOR

CHAPTER OBJECTIVE

After completing this chapter, the reader will be able to describe how humor can affect the immune system, physiological health, and pain management.

LEARNING OBJECTIVES

After studying this chapter, the reader will be able to

1. articulate the body's normal response to stress.
2. identify the immunological changes caused by humor.
3. describe how humor may affect cardiac and respiratory well-being.
4. discuss the brain's response to humor.
5. describe the use of humor as an adjunct therapy in pain management.

PHYSIOLOGICAL STRESS REACTION

Stressful life events cause the autonomic nervous system to prepare for "fight or flight." The body's physiological stress reaction is diagrammed in Figure 3-1.

When a person experiences acute physical or emotional stress, the adrenal gland increases its secretion of cortisol. Increased heart rate and blood pressure enhance blood flow to the skeletal muscles, enabling the person to flee the situation. The cortisol increase also increases appetite. As a result, fat breaks down to provide energy to the muscles. Production of dehydroepiandrosterone (DHEA), a steroid that helps buffer the body against the effects of excess cortisol, also increases. This buffer works as a protective mechanism during times of acute stress.

When a person perceives a threat, real or imagined, the body activates the general adaptation syndrome (GAS). During the alarm reaction of the GAS, the hypothalamus-pituitary-adrenal (HPA) axis is activated. The anterior pituitary gland releases adrenocorticotropic hormone (ACTH) which, in turn, increases the secretion of cortisol from the adrenal gland into the systemic circulation. A complex feedback mechanism within the immune and endocrine systems works to further regulate HPA function, preventing excessive secretion of cortisol and ACTH. Epinephrine and norepinephrine are released due to stimulation of the adrenal medulla. The heart rate is raised and the blood vessels constrict.

Also known as the *stress response,* fight-or-flight syndrome worked well when humans were hunters and gatherers. It allowed the body to quickly change from quiet waiting to a rapid physical response. However, emotional stress causes overstimulation of the HPA axis and can lead to physiological changes that have detrimental effects on the body. With long periods of stress, DHEA levels fall,

FIGURE 3-1: PHYSIOLOGICAL STRESS REACTION

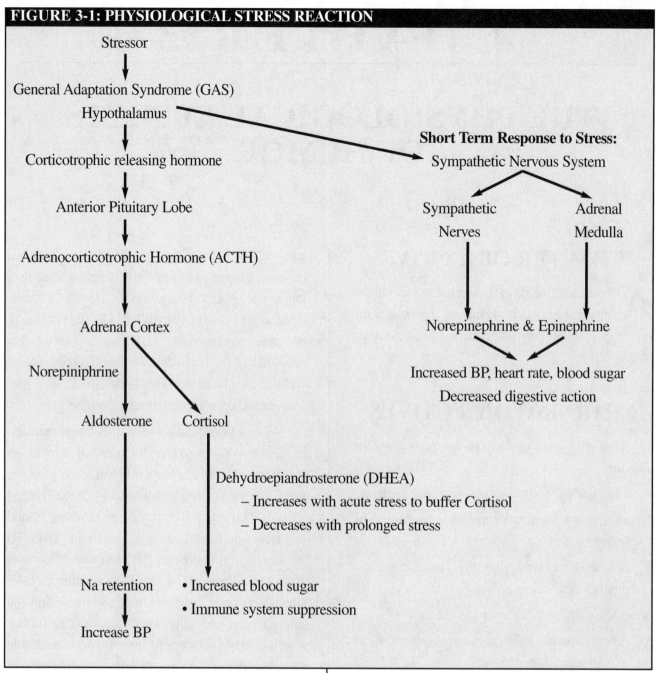

leaving high cortisol levels unchecked. High levels of cortisol can create immunosuppression, leaving the body more susceptible to infection and disease.

When an individual experiences a stressful life event, his or her muscles become tense. The person may develop a headache, clench the jaw, grind the teeth, or experience tightness in the neck, shoulder, and back muscles. The digestive system is affected and loss of appetite, abdominal discomfort, nausea, vomiting, diarrhea, and irritable bowel syndrome may occur. Tension can also lead to heart attacks.

Ford-Martin (2001) notes that 80% to 90% of all diseases are believed to be stress related.

Risk factors for stress-related illnesses include a mix of personal, interpersonal, and social variables. These factors can include lack or loss of social support or an actual or perceived loss of control over one's physical environment. A stress response can occur with negative life events, such as the death of loved one or loss of a job. It can also occur with life events that are viewed as positive, such as getting married, attending finishing school, becoming a parent, or entering into retirement. It has also been found that people who are dependent on others, such as children or the elderly, and those who are socially disadvantaged because of race, gender, educational level, or similar factors are at great risk for developing stress-related diseases (Ford-Martin, 2001).

IMMUNE RESPONSE TO HUMOR

Many research studies have been conducted on the immunological effects of humor. Some researchers, however, are concerned with the methodology used (Martin, 2001). This research has been criticized for inadequate sample sizes and other methodological weaknesses. Although the scientific evidence is inadequate to state with certainty that response to humor can cause changes in the immune system, these studies do provide clues to how humor can affect the immune system and can be used to design further research studies with stronger statistical significance. From a nursing perspective, it is important to ask, "Is it worth trying something fun that might help boost immune function?"

A quick review of immune system properties that may be affected by humor can help you to understand how humor can be used in health care (see Table 3-1). Research indicates that humor increases the immunoglobulin IgA. Studies also indicate that IgG, IgM, killer T cells, and natural killer (NK) cells increase with laughter (Berk et al., 1989; Berk, Felten, Tan, Bittman, & Westengard, 2001). Sedimentation rate and the amount of cortisol in blood reportedly decrease as a result of laughter. All of these effects have potential benefits for patients.

One of the best-known studies that examined the immunological effects of humor and laughter was conducted by Berk and associates in 1989 and was replicated in 1993. Although there are some questions about methodology regarding control groups (Martin, 2001), these studies indicate that

humor has some definite immunological benefits. The following points summarize the effects of humor on the immune system according to the studies of Berk and associates:

- IgG increases with hearty laughter and remains elevated for 24 hours.

- IgA and IgM also increase, and levels stay elevated into the next day.

- Mirthful laughter increases NK cell activity and increases the actual number of cells.

- Gamma interferon increases two-fold as subjects watch a humor video.

Along with changes in the amounts of IgA, IgG, IgM, T cells, and NK cells, cortisol secretion decreased. As cortisol increases in the body, immune defenses decrease. Therefore, a decrease in cortisol should increase the immune system's ability to respond. The level of B cells also increased when subjects watched a comedy video. This result is not surprising because B cells are responsible for the production of immunoglobulins.

Another study of ten students revealed a significant increase in salivary IgA after students viewed a humorous videotape (Groves, 1991). This study on salivary IgA and perceived mood over a number of weeks revealed that IgA concentrations were high on days the subjects perceived they were in a positive mood. On days the individuals perceived themselves to be in a negative mood, the salivary concentrations were lower. Another interesting finding was that IgA levels were "directly related to the subjects' perceptions of their use of humor as a coping device" (Groves, 1991, p. 52). Those who viewed themselves as using humor as a coping device did not have as high an increase in IgA after viewing the humorous film as those who did not use humor as a coping device.

Another IgA study indicated that those who watched a laughter film did not have higher levels of immunoglobulins (Martin, 2001). However, this same study revealed that humor had a direct relation-

TABLE 3-1: IMMUNE SYSTEM PROPERTIES AND FUNCTIONS	
Property	**Location and Function**
Immunoglobulins	Respond to antigen release, such as bacteria and viruses
IgG	Major immunoglobulin in blood. Coats microorganisms and speeds their uptake by cells in the immune system. Responsible for producing long-term immunity.
IgA	Found in saliva, tears, secretions of gastrointestinal and respiratory tracts and guard entrances to the body to protect against colds and flu.
IgM	Found in bloodstream. First antibody to arrive during hormonal response. Kills bacteria.
Complement 3	Helps antibodies penetrate and destroy defective or infective cells
T cells	Help organize immune system responses
Helper T	Mobilize many immune cells, especially B and T cells.
Killer T cells	Fight off invading organisms, especially viruses and cells transformed by cancer
Suppressor T cells	Help stop T cell reaction when T cells are no longer needed
Phagocytes	White blood cells that engulf and digest foreign invaders
B cells	Produced by the bone marrow. Generate antibodies to fight potentially harmful microorganisms.
Natural Killer (NK) cells	Attack viruses and tumor cells
Cytokines	Small proteins that are released from cells. Act as messengers to other cells. Actively involved in the immune response
Gamma interferon	Specialized hormone-like product. Regulates anticellular activities and turns on mononuclear lymphocytes (white blood cells)

ship with participants' perceptions of their use of humor as a coping mechanism. Those who said they used humor to cope had higher baseline levels of IgA.

Berk and colleagues (2001) refer to the type of stress that is modulated by humor as *eustress*. Wanting to discover the immune parameters affected by mirthful laughter, they designed a study to look at specific immunological effects of laughter. They did a series of five separate studies using 52 healthy men who viewed a humor video of their choice for 1 hour. Blood samples were taken before, during, and after the intervention. The control group rested comfortably and had access to a number of magazines. Their results showed specific immunologic effects of laughter (see Table 3-2).

A study by Bennett, Zeller, Rosenberg, and McCann (2003) found that people who scored high on the Humor Response Scale (HRS) had higher levels of NK cell activity than those who did not. When participants were exposed to a humor video but did not respond with mirthful laughter, NK cell activity seemed unaffected. However, those individuals who experienced mirthful laughter and scored high on the HRS had increased levels of NK cell activity. The researchers concluded that "because of the role of NK cells in viral illness and various types of cancer, the ability to significantly increase NK cell activity in a brief period of time using a noninvasive method could be clinically important" (Bennett et al., 2003, p. 43). Using humor to stimu-

TABLE 3-2: EFFECTS OF HUMOR AND LAUGHTER ON IMMUNE SYSTEM

Immune System Component	Effects on Immune System
Natural Killer Cells (NK)	Increase activity, especially in experimental subjects
IgG, IgA, IgM	Increased after 30 minutes, remain elevated 90 minutes and 12 hours after intervention
Complement 3	Significant increase after 90 minutes after intervention
T-cells	Increase activity during intervention and remain for at least 90 minutes
B-cells	Increases significantly at 90 minutes and remain up to 12 hours
Helper T cells	Increase during intervention, remain elevated up to 12 hours
Cytokine Gamma Interferon	Significant increase at 90 minutes and remains elevated up to 12 hours
Total leukocytes	Increased during and 90 minutes after intervention

late laughter might improve NK cell activity in those with viral illness or cancer.

OTHER PHYSIOLOGICAL EFFECTS OF HUMOR

Think about what happens when someone laughs:

- The person takes in big breaths of air, and then blows them out.
- The stomach moves and perhaps the person's whole body begins to move.
- If the person laughs very hard, his or her face may turn red.

All of this activity that occurs with laughter may have some important physiological benefits. For example, a postoperative patient who laughs at the antics of a hospital clown laughs, coughs, and then laughs again at the clown's antics. The coughing helps clear the lungs, and the laughter is much more fun than using an incentive spirometer.

In an interview with Patty Wooten (1994), Dr. Fry stated that laughter "disturbed the usual pattern of respiration, increased the minute volume, and created a forceful exhalation which could mobilize secretions." Laughter is believed to work on the respiratory system by triggering a bellows action on the thoracic cavity. Laughter did not, however, increase oxygen saturation. Fry also noted that laughter aids ventilation and the cleansing of mucus from the lungs. This finding might help those with certain chronic respiratory conditions. Plus, large muscle masses are activated during laughter, which creates a total body response that may be useful in providing conditioning exercises for bed-ridden or wheelchair-bound patients.

Consider the dissection of laughter by Kuhn (2003). He talks about 15 stages of laughter (see Table 3-3). While reading about each stage, think about what part of the body is being exercised.

Berk (2002) notes that 15 facial muscles are used with a hearty guffaw, and the skeletal muscles contract. Laughter creates a total body response. Berk (2002) mentions that a belly laugh exercises the chest and abdominal muscles, improving their tone. This exercise can be important for wheelchair-bound or bed-ridden patients. Use of the abdominal muscles during hearty laughter can also affect the gastrointestinal system and may improve digestion. During laughter, normal cyclic breathing is disrupted, ventilation increases, mucus plugs may clear, and residual air exchange is accelerated. Increased pulmonary ventilation results in blowing off excess carbon dioxide and water vapor that builds up in residual air. Fry contends that laughter allows more

TABLE 3-3: 15 STAGES OF LAUGHTER

1. **Smirk:** This is the often fleeting, slight upturning of the corners of the mouth and a gentle hint of openness in the eyes. It is completely voluntary and controlled. It is commonly hard to detect.

2. **Smile:** This is usually voluntary, silent, controlled, and easily noticed. The corners of the mouth turn upward and the eyes sparkle.

3. **Grin:** This is also silent and controlled but uses more facial muscles. The corners of the mouth are stretched upward, and the cheeks are involved.

4. **Snicker:** This involves the first emergence of sound accompanied by facial movement. It is accompanied by sounds caused by bursts of air released from the nose.

5. **Giggle:** This usually tickles us inside and is expressed outwardly in sound.It involves a series of rapid, often high-pitched sounds. The sound of giggling can be amusing. The attempt to suppress it tends to increase its strength.

6. **Chuckle:** This involves the chest muscles, and the sound has a deeper pitch. The sound is similar "to a dog whose bark is caught in his throat" (Kuhn, 2003, p. 36). The sound seems to come from the back of the throat.

7. **Chortle:** This response originates deeper in the chest and involves the torso muscles. It usually provokes laughter in others.

8. **Laugh:** By the time the process reaches the laugh, it is irreversible. The laugh involves facial and thoracic muscles as well as the abdomen and extremities. Sounds of barking or snorting may occur.

9. **Cackle:** At this point, the process is involuntary. The pitch of the sound is higher, the body begins to rock, the spine extends and flexes, and the head becomes upturned. Kuhn (2003) refers to this sound as "a laugh on pep pills."

10. **Guffaw:** At this stage, the whole body responds. Feet stomp, arms wave, and the person may slap his or her thighs. The torso rocks and the sound that emerges is deep and loud. "It is incompatible with a full bladder" (Kuhn, 2003, pg. 37).

11. **Howl:** The body becomes more animated as the volume and pitch rise higher and higher.

12. **Shriek:** The intensity increases. There is a sense of vulnerability and helplessness.

13. **Roar:** By this time, the audience is also roaring. Individuality is lost.

14. **Convulse:** The body is completely out of control in a fit of laughter that resembles a seizure. Extremities flail aimlessly. The person loses balance, starts gasping for breath, and collapses or falls off the chair.

15. **Die laughing:** This is a brief, physically intense experience in which there is a instant of total helplessness. It is a transcendent experience. The person is totally powerless, defenseless, and incapable of purposeful movement. After the experience, it is as if the person is reborn.

> You have nothing left . . . Like a newborn infant, you may be physically weak and lack coordination. All of your senses may be refreshed and sharpened. And, in some instances, you may need a change of underwear (Kuhn, 2003, p. 38).

(Kuhn, 2003)

oxygen availability for red blood cell uptake in addition to decreasing moisture, thereby preventing pulmonary bacterial growth (Berk, 2002).

Lebowitz (2002) conducted two studies to investigate the effects of humor on patients with COPD. The first study was a humor intervention study where 22 participants were shown either a humorous or a neutral video presentation. The following concerns were evaluated before and after the intervention: pulmonary function, blood pressure, heart rate, affect and anxiety. The results of this study indicated that those individuals who viewed the humorous film had problems with increased air trapped in their lungs. An interesting finding is that patients with less severe pulmonary disease tended to have more air trapping following the humor intervention than individuals with more severe disease. The results indicated that laughter might affect pulmonary functioning by causing acute increases in functional residual capacity.

The second study by Lebowitz (2002) was concerned with the psychological and health benefits related to a sense of humor and the use of humor as a coping mechanism for patients with COPD. This sample contained 46 participants. The study revealed that a humorous coping style decreased depression, diminished anxiety, decreased negative affect, and enhanced the person's quality of life. Those with a humorous coping style also had fewer infections. The author concludes that those persons with a humorous coping style experience psychological and health related benefits. However, the act of laughing aloud may cause negative pulmonary functioning. The results of these studies indicate that humor should be used cautiously with patients who have COPD.

Twenty-six men and women in Japan were exposed to allergens resulting in an allergic response (Maranan, 2001). The allergens were dust mites, cedar pollen, and cat dander (PRIMEDIA Intertec, 2001). The subjects were then shown a Charlie Chaplin film. Following the film, the symptoms in all 26 participants were reduced for 4 hours. This same procedure was done with patients viewing a video with weather information. The second group showed no relief after the viewing. Although the study does not have statistical significance because the study group was very small, it does demonstrate that laughter *might* be one way of decreasing allergic symptoms in some people.

Dr. Fry decided to investigate the effect of laughter. Dr. Fry believes that venous return is enhanced partly by the milking action of active muscles on the venous system (Wooten, 1994). Laughter initially causes an increase in heart rate, blood pressure, and respiratory rate. It also works the face and stomach muscles and relaxes muscles that are not involved in laughing (Dossey, 1996). Using himself as a subject, Fry found that one minute of hearty laughter brought his heart rate up to the same level as 10 minutes of rowing on his home rowing machine. Which would be more enjoyable: hearty laughter or rowing for 10 minutes?

Tan, Tan, Berk, Lukman, and Lukman (1997) investigated the effect of humor on patients who experienced myocardial infarctions (MIs). Researchers followed two groups of patients for 1 year of cardiac rehabilitation. The experimental group viewed self-selected humor for 30 minutes per day as an adjunct to the standard cardiac therapy. The control group was not directed to view humor. The study showed that patients who viewed the humor had fewer episodes of arrhythmias, lower blood pressure, lower urinary and plasma catecholamines, less need for beta blockers and nitroglycerin, and a lower incidence of recurrent MI than the control group.

According to the University of Maryland Medical Center (Laughter Helps, 2005), a recent study indicates that emotions appear to have an effect on the inner lining of blood vessels, the endothelium. Viewing a movie that provoked laughter had the effect of dilating blood vessels and increasing blood flow. In contrast, viewing movie clips that tended to cause mental stress resulted in a decreased brachial artery flow. The study was unable to determine the source of laughter's benefit. It might be caused by the movement of the diaphragm muscles when a person chuckles or guffaws, or a chemical release triggered by the laughter. Whatever the cause, the researchers believe this study adds to the evidence that there is a connection between laughter and cardiovascular health.

In another study, 150 men and women with histories of either coronary revascularization or MI were evaluated using a self-rating questionnaire that measured tendency to laugh in a number of different circumstances (Jancin, 2001). Their questionnaires were compared to a control group of 150 healthy adults of the same ages. The results showed that individuals who had heart disease were less likely to use humor as an adaptive mechanism during difficult situations. They were also less likely to use humor in daily activities, surprise situations, and social interactions. They were also less likely to use laughter during positive experiences or in general. This study indicates that a good sense of humor may be cardioprotective (Jancin, 2001). In an article mentioning this study, Walsh (n.d.) notes that researchers think a "laugh might help keep hearts healthy by helping to decrease blood vessel inflammation, decreasing the risk of clots, or helping to maintain normal blood pressure levels" (¶3).

An interesting study conducted on 19 patients with type 2 diabetes suggests that a significant suppression of 2-hour postprandial blood glucose (PPBG) level occurred after watching a comedy show (Hayashi et al., 2003). As noted by the authors, negative emotions, such as fear, anxiety, or sorrow, tend to elevate blood glucose levels. The results of this study indicate that laughter has an inhibitory effect on the increase in PPBG. The reason for this effect is not clear, but Hayashi et al. (2003) have two different theories for this phenomenon: (1) the acceleration of glucose used by the muscle motion while laughing and (2) positive emotions, such as laughter, act on the neuroendocrine system and suppress the elevation of blood glucose levels. Because this is probably the first study conducted on blood glucose and the sample size was small, more studies need to be done.

One word of caution: Some people have experienced negative physiological effects to laughter (Berk et al., 2001). A small number of people experience neurological reactions to laughter. These reactions include seizures and cataleptic and narcoleptic attacks. Following abdominal surgery or pelvic surgery, laughter may be contraindicated because increased abdominal and thoracic pressure can occur. This increase in pressure can also have negative consequences for those with respiratory diseases such as asthma.

THE BRAIN'S RESPONSE

In an interview for *Humor & Health Letter* (Humor in the brain, 1995), Dr. Peter Derks, Professor of Psychology at the College of William and Mary, shared the following information:

- Changes occur in the brain when a person really laughs at an event they find funny as opposed to reading a joke that does not elicit laughter. This might relate to some kind of releaser process. This electric response in the brain may stimulate the endocrine responses that Berk and Tan found in their studies.

- Response to humor involves both of the brain's hemispheres. The left hemisphere (the one involved with language) sets up the joke. The right hemisphere (the one involved in pattern recognition and processing simultaneous information) is activated when we "get the joke."

- When a person reads a joke, the left hemisphere of the brain is active. The response, however, instantaneously activates the whole cortex. Derks states, "As the process continues, the left hemisphere begins to shut down, and the right picks up. Then both hemispheres join in a sort of holistic dance" (p. 26).

- Humor involves the whole person and all information processing abilities — cognition, emotion, feelings, and ideas.

Strubbe (2003) explains that, although the left side understands puns, complex non-word-play jokes are processed by the right-side gyri, which then triggers activity in other parts of the brain. Doskoch (1996) notes that about "four-tenths of a second after we hear the punch line of a joke — but before we laugh — a negatively charged wave of electricity sweeps through the cortex"(¶3). This electrical wave, which can be seen on an EEG, eventually covers the entire cerebral cortex. The brain's response to laughter differs from emotional responses in that emotional responses are mainly the function of the frontal lobe, whereas laughter occurs in the left, front, right, and rear of the cerebral cortex as well as in the motor section of the brain.

Another chance to explore brain-driven laughter occurred at the University of California at Los Angeles (UCLA) Medical Center with a young, seizure-prone woman (Strubbe, 2003). When a restricted area of the woman's left frontal cortex was electrically stimulated, she laughed consistently and perceived whatever she was looking at as funny. Low levels of stimulation made her smile. Higher levels of stimulation lead to belly laughter. Perhaps the future will provide more information on the physiological effects of laughter and the use of methods other than medication to decrease depression.

HUMOR AND PAIN MANAGEMENT

When you're hungry, sing; when you're hurt, laugh.
Jewish Proverb

Interest in the effects of laughter on pain control arose after Norman Cousins (1979) shared his experience of using humor to control his pain level during his recovery from ankylosing spondylitis. Cousins found that he could control his pain by reading humorous books and watching Marx Brothers films and *Candid Camera* productions. He found that 10 minutes of belly laughter left him pain free for about 2 hours.

Like humor, pain is a perception. This perception affects people's emotions. If the mind and body are inseparable, then one cannot feel pain physiologically without some emotional effect. It is known that pain is changeable and variable. Different people perceive pain differently depending on past experiences with pain, cultural expectations of pain, the meaning of a situation to that person (some people are incapacitated by pain and others might just find it annoying), and other stressors affecting tension within the body.

The actual physiological process that affects the pain level following laughter is still not known. It is believed that laughter helps by providing a distraction, reducing tension, changing expectations, and possibly increasing production of endogenous endorphins — the body's own morphine (Rosner, 2002). The belief that endorphins are released has not been demonstrated in research studies according to the literature search conducted for this text.

A number of controlled studies used a noxious stimuli during the viewing of humorous material to determine if laughter had any effect on pain levels (Provine, 2000a). The noxious stimulation included a mild electric current applied to participants' forearms, blood pressure cuff inflation, or cold-pressor tasks (such as placing the hands in ice water). The end results of these controlled studies indicated that pain threshold is increased with laughter. There is also speculation that mirthful laughter increases endorphins; however, so far, no definitive studies support this belief (Martin, 2001).

One study reported by Provine (2000a) found that participants who watched a humorous video while having their hand in ice water could endure the pain. The funnier they perceived the video, the longer they could endure the pain. The control group in this study viewed a documentary. The control group experienced the same amount of pain relief. This finding led to the conclusion that distraction, or a related cognitive process, contributed to the pain relief.

In a field study involving 26 females diagnosed with rheumatoid arthritis, researchers found that there was a significant decrease in self-reported pain ratings after watching a 1-hour performance of rakugo, a form of Japanese humor. Another study of 13 elderly residents in a long-term care facility indicated that the amount of pain medication used to manage their chronic pain decreased after watching a comedy.

Leise (1993) conducted a study of 30 women between the ages of 33 and 66 who had a diagnosis of rheumatoid arthritis and no other chronic problems. The study examined the relationship between chronic pain and a healthy sense of humor. Individuals who reported a high level of pain also reported using humor frequently. Leise (1993) noted that individuals who experience a lot of pain may need a lot of humor in their lives to cope. This study did not indicate that humor helped control the pain, but it did indicate that those experiencing chronic pain may need more humor to cope with the stress of the pain.

Mahony, Burroughs, and Hieatt (2001) discuss a number of studies that looked at the use of humor during painful or uncomfortable interventions. One test involved blood pressure cuffs, another a transcutaneous end nerve stimulation, and another a cold-water pressor. The summation of these studies is that having a sense of humor trait is more beneficial than an induced humor state, and it appears that laughter's benefit to pain management is its ability to cause relaxation or distraction.

Mahony and colleagues (2001) became interested in discovering if expectation of the benefit from laughter or from relaxation would have an effect on pain threshold. Their study involved 50 male and 84 female undergraduate students. Participants were assigned to either a humor or a relaxation exposure group. Students were randomly assigned to groups and given instructions concerning the benefits or the nonbenefits of humor and discomfort. All the participants except the control group were told that the video they would be watching would either increase or decrease their sensitivity to the discomfort caused by an inflated blood pressure cuff. One group watched a humorous video without being given instructions about expectations. The relaxation group watched a video about Hawaii. The laughter group watched an episode of "Seinfeld." The researchers concluded that an induced humor state is no more effective than induced relaxation when it comes to coping with discomfort. The researchers do say that "it is fairly safe to assume that most people in pain would prefer a laughter intervention, particularly one of their own choosing, over relaxation exercises, hypnotism, or reading a brochure arguing the benefits of a particular program" (¶17). More studies are needed. As Mahony and colleagues (2001) note, although the effects of laughter may not be quantitatively superior to the effects of relaxation, distraction, or expectations on pain control, it is possible that laughter is qualitatively superior in some way.

One study cited by Mahony and colleagues (2001) looked at the response of 78 postsurgical patients who were either part of a control group or one of eight experimental groups. One group watched either a comedy or an action/adventure video. One group was given a choice of videos or no video, and one group was either the positive expectation or no expectation group. Expectation was formed by having the appropriate group read an article describing the benefits of either a comedy or an exciting movie. Patients who viewed the comedy took lower doses of minor pain medication than those who watched the action/adventure videos. Those given a choice of comedy videos needed lower doses of medication than those who did not have a choice. Those given a choice of action videos showed no effect of choice. This study indicates that humor preference is individual and that few things are as irritating as exposure to material that does not appear to be funny to that individual.

Adams and McGuire (1986) studied the effect of laughter on an older population residing in a long-term care facility. This was a small study of 13 subjects. Seven of the subjects watched a humorous movie and six members watched a nonhumorous movie. Originally, the researchers planned on using the McGill Pain Assessment Questionnaire, but this survey proved too lengthy for the subjects. Instead, pain perceptions were evaluated subjectively. Therefore, the study did not evaluate the use of humor on pain perception statistically. Most of the humor group residents claimed to have less pain at the end of the program. However, the statements of less pain might have occurred as a means of trying to please the researchers. This study needs replication to assess its validity.

The UCLA Children's Hospital has started a program called Rx Laughter to try and ease sick children through multiple medical procedures and minimize the traumatic effects the children experience (Rx Laughter, 2002). The program is a collaboration between pediatrics, psychiatry, and the entertainment industry. As well as offering a diversion for children, this program looks at the behaviors and thoughts generated by the laughter. One area of interest is the relationship between humor, laughter, pain perception, and pain tolerance. So far, the study indicates that watching a comedy during a procedure is more effective for pain management than watching a comedy video before the procedure.

SUMMARY

Although many studies are controversial because of limited sample sizes and research methodologies, there is evidence that humor positively affects the immune response. Studies also show that humor affects the cardiac and respiratory systems. Some positive correlations between pain manage-

ment and the use of humor therapy also exist. Many studies have measured the physiological effects of humor and laughter, but more research is needed.

EXAM QUESTIONS

CHAPTER 3
Questions 19-27

19. The body's physiological response during acute stress is

    a. reduced secretion of cortisol.

    b. reduced heart rate and BP.

    c. suppression of epinephrine.

    d. increased secretion of cortisol.

20. Humor increases the level of

    a. ACTH.

    b. DHEA.

    c. IgA.

    d. norepinephrine.

21. The immunoglobulin that increases with humor and is responsible for producing long-term immunity is

    a. IgA.

    b. IgG.

    c. IgM.

    d. IgB.

22. NK cells are activated by the body to attack

    a. tumor cells.

    b. *Pseudomonas.*

    c. *Streptococcus.*

    d. *Staphylococcus.*

23. Laughter may be one way to improve respiratory function after surgery because it

    a. decreases pulmonary ventilation.

    b. relaxes chest and abdominal muscles.

    c. triggers a bellows action on the thoracic cavity.

    d. decreases oxygen saturation.

24. The results of Lebowitz studies (2002) indicate that when caring for patients with COPD, nurses should use humor that leads to laughter

    a. as often as possible.

    b. cautiously.

    c. never.

    d. periodically.

25. When someone hears and understands a joke

    a. the left side of the brain is activated.

    b. the right side of the brain is activated.

    c. both brain hemispheres are activated.

    d. neuronal firing occurs.

26. In studies, immunological responses seem to vary depending on a person's perception of a comedy video because humor preference is

    a. individual.

    b. learned.

    c. predictable.

    d. important.

27. According to one study cited by Mahony (2001), when postsurgical patients were given a choice of the comedy videos they wanted to watch, their need for pain medication

    a. increased.

    b. decreased.

    c. stayed the same.

    d. varied.

CHAPTER 4

PSYCHOSOCIAL EFFECTS OF HUMOR

CHAPTER OBJECTIVE

After completing this chapter the reader will be able to discuss the psychosocial effects of humor.

LEARNING OBJECTIVES

After studying this chapter, the reader will be able to

1. describe how humor works as a form of social communication.

2. discuss how humor can be used to handle negative feelings or events.

3. describe how humor works to relieve stress.

4. identify potential gender differences in responses to humor and laughter.

5. discuss the efficacy of humor in end-of-life care

HUMOR AS SOCIAL COMMUNICATION

A smile is the shortest distance between two people.

Victor Borge

Communication is one of the functions of humor. Robinson (1991) states that it is not a formal communication mode, but a casual, indirect form of communication. Humor helps communicate feelings, thoughts, and beliefs to others in a way that might be difficult to convey using other means of communica-

tion. Humor can be used to diffuse feelings of anger or impatience by pointing out the absurdity of the situational threat to the ego (Goodman, 2002; Salameh, 1983; Seaward, 1992). Shared humor can help dispel fear and provide a clearer focus on the situation. Humor appears to communicate feelings of fear in a way that diminishes stress in an acceptable manner (Seaward, 1992).

Humor can be an element in effective interpersonal communication (Lippert, 2001). Humor helps dissolve barriers between individuals. As Seaward (1994, cited in Dossey, 1996) noted, "humor has an adhesive quality, which connects and bonds people together, if only for the duration of a joke." Gullickson (1995) talks about how humor can communicate a patient's feelings or concerns that may go beyond words. If nurses listen to the feelings behind patients' words, therapeutic interventions can be used to help diffuse the tension patients might be feeling. Gullickson (1995) shares an example about a nurse working with a patient about to undergo a kidney transplant. The nurse was preparing the patient for the transplant. When the nurse asked if there was anything the patient wanted to talk about, the patient responded, "Well, you know, it's not like I'm going to die or anything," and then he started to laugh (Gullickson, 1995, p. 20). The nurse had the sense that there were fears behind the attempted humor that were unspeakable. She responded, "You know, I think we need to talk about that" (Gullickson, 1995, p. 21). The nurse's ability to hear the concerns behind the patient's words and laughter, and her comfort in responding to the underlying issues, allowed this patient to discuss his fears and emotional issues that needed attention.

The nurse in the previous example may have realized that laughter is not always the result of humor. People sometimes laugh because they are nervous or angry and do not want to express these emotions. In other cases, people laugh because they think it is the thing to do, such as when someone tells a joke and another person does not understand but convention says that it is impolite not to laugh so the person laughs, or the person laughs because he or she does not want the other person to think he or she is dumb.

Henman (2001) notes that "communication humor" has been associated with personality traits such as "extroversion, lower anxiety, internal locus of control, and field independence" (p. 90). Henman mentions that there is a positive relationship between humor and expressivity. Those who can use humor effectively present a positive impression.

The importance of humor in social interactions begins in childhood. A study by Sobstad (cited in Fuhr, 2002) found that children who had no humor were likely to play alone. Humor seems to be an important element in social acceptance for status within a group of peers. Other studies have demonstrated that boys who have the highest status among their peers were likely to be the most frequent users of jocular phrases, jokes, and remarks with implicit sexual references (Fuhr, 2002).

Humor and shared laughter can add to feelings of togetherness, warmth, friendliness, and closeness (Astedt-Kurki & Isola, 2001). Humor and laughter can convey a sense of connection between individuals. Social humor may aid in the establishment and development of relationships (Conkell, Imwold, & Ratliffe, 1999). Humor that connects one person to another can help diffuse a stressful situation. Humor used for stress reduction can be seen in the healthcare setting. For example, when a nurse offers a

preoperative patient a hospital gown and says, "Please put on our Paris original." The joking attitude can help ease some of the patient's anxiety.

Provine (2000a) discovered that laughter occurred 30 times more frequently in social situations than solitary situations. This observation was obtained by watching university students' interactions with instructors and with other students. Many of the statements that resulted in laughter were not jokes, but simple statements between individuals, such as "You don't have to drink; just buy us drinks!" Laughter is a signal we send to others. The response of laughter to something mildly humorous seems to disappear when we do not have an audience.

Humor can be used as an interpersonal means of providing comfort. Frecknall (1994) found that the participants in his study felt that humor provided a closeness with others. In a qualitative study by Beck (1997), one theme that emerged was that humor provided an effective therapeutic communication technique that helped to decrease patient anxiety. In a study by Bippus (2000) on humor usage in comforting, all participants were able to recall an interaction in which a friend's use of humor provided an element of comfort during a stressful situation. Humor appears to flow between those who are close, providing an element of release and comfort in times of distress. What happens when the comforter is a stranger, such as in the healthcare setting?

Care providers often attempt to find ways of comforting others (Bippus, 2000). Robinson (1991) notes that humor that "quickly provides a sense of familiarity, does not offend, and is easily facilitated" (p. 51) helps to build a trusting relationship between healthcare providers and patients. Lippert (2001) discovered that humor was an essential part of the relationship between nurses and long-term care residents. Joking tends to strengthen bonds between patients and nurses. An example of this occurred during admission of a same-day surgery patient. The patient had been a regular at the hospital prior to the admission nurse's experience with him. He was an obese man with a reputation for being "obnoxious and difficult." The nurse entered the patient's room with the hospital gown and made a comment about putting on the "Paris original." The patient chuckled and made a humorous comment in response about the gown not covering anything. This interchange established a comfortable relationship between the patient and nurse. As a result, the patient cooperated with the pre-operative procedure and was able to share with the nurse his concerns about having surgery.

Gender and Social Hierarchy

An interesting question exists about the differences between the use of humor and humor appreciation between men and women. Is there really a difference? Research does not support a difference in the effects of humor on coping (Abel, 1998). However, response to humor and humor preferences do appear to have some gender-related differences (Provine, 2000b; Robinson & Smith-Lovin, 2001).

A study by Robinson and Smith-Lovin (2001) reports that men tell more jokes than women do. Women joke more with each other when men are not present. Men use humor as a hierarchy-building method. This study indicates that, during group meetings, group members with higher status use more humor and get more laughs than those with lower status. This response seems to support the superiority theory of humor.

Provine (2000b) noticed that women laughed about 126% more than men. Men tended to be the producers of humor. Looking at personal advertisements, Provine noticed that women tended to look for partners with a sense of humor, whereas men were more likely to offer humor. One conclusion Provine (2000b) made by reviewing his study results and studies of others is that the laughter of women, rather than of men, is the critical index of a healthy relationship.

HUMOR AS A COPING STRATEGY AND STRESS RELIEVER

The crisis of today is the joke of tomorrow.
H.G. Wells

Stress is commonly the result of "stinkin' thinkin'." Much of the stress people feel comes from the way they perceive events. When viewing the following, what do you see?

Opportunityisnowhere?

Do you see "Opportunity is nowhere?" Or do you see "Opportunity is now here?" How do you perceive the message?

The meaning an individual places on a situation influences how the person feels about the situation. If a person tells himself or herself that a certain event is terrible, he or she will react to that stressor in a negative manner. A person's reaction to stress may manifest itself physically, psychologically, socially, and even spiritually. Emotionally, stress can manifest as moodiness, inability to concentrate, irritability, changes in eating or sleeping patterns, crying, decreased libido, worrying, mood swings, frustration, nervousness, and depression. Individuals may also display a negative attitude, lack of creativity, lethargy, low productivity, confusion, boredom, or forgetfulness (Buxman, 1998). They may isolate themselves from others or feel a sense of loneliness. Preoccupation with stressful events can lead to negative mood swings, lashing out at others, nagging, or distancing oneself from and not talking to others.

Lefcourt and Martin (1986) believe that humor and laughter are "an important mechanism for coping with many of the psychological stressors that humans encounter in their daily lives" (p. 1). It is believed that humor helps to decrease the sense of stress by producing a cognitive shift or by helping to restructure how a person views a situation (Abel, 1998). In other words, humor provides a different perspective on stressful situations. It gives people a sense of control over their environments and offers a sense of self-protection (Wooten, 1996). Humor helps people view stressful situations in more positive and challenging ways by helping to refocus attention on less-negative aspects of the situation (Kuiper, Martin, & Olinger, 1993). One of the themes from Frecknell's (1994) qualitative study was that "humor provides significant and often unexpected release from stress" (p. 17).

How negative life events impact individuals depends on such variables as coping strategies and hardiness (Porterfield, 1987). Wooten (1996) refers to the issue of internal versus external locus of control. Individuals with external locuses of control believe that things happen to them that are beyond their control. Those who have internal locuses of control believe they have some control over what happens to them; these people are more likely to take control of their own healthcare. Wooten's (1996) study indicated that individuals who were encouraged to use humor developed a sense of control in their lives. This sense of control made individuals more willing to follow recommended health interventions. Wooten (1997) mentioned that her observations led her to believe that patients with good sense of humor or playful spirits have a resilience and strength that helps them deal with the difficult and frightening moments of illness.

Martin and Lefcourt (1983) designed three quantitative studies using different measures of sense of humor and its effect on moderating the impact of stressful events. All three studies provided initial evidence that humor played a role in buffering stress (Martin & Lefcourt, 1983). The researchers also found an inverse relationship between humor production and life stressors and between humor production and negative mood. Plus, subjects who reported high stress levels also reported producing and using more humor.

The first study by Martin and Lefcourt (1983) used three different humor assessment tools, each of which measured somewhat different aspects of the complex sense of humor constructs. The researchers used the Life Events of College Students and Profile of Mood States questionnaires to determine level of stress and feelings of tension, depression, anger, fatigue, and confusion. This study indicated that individuals who tend to smile and laugh in a wide variety of situations place a high value on the use of humor, and those who state they use humor as a means of coping with stressful events have less pronounced mood disturbance from the effects of stress. The second study, which used a self-report measure of sense of humor, also indicated that humor had a stress-buffering effect. The same result was evident in the third study, in which participants were instructed to make up humorous statements for a silent film and then complete a questionnaire. This study indicated that neither the ability to accurately perceive humorous stimuli in one's environment nor reports of humor appreciation were significant for humor to decrease or moderate the effect of stress. However, those who placed a high value on humor for handling difficult situations and were able to produce humorous stories demonstrated significantly lower levels of mood disturbances.

Since the 1983 study by Martin and Lefcourt, other quantitative studies on the use of humor have demonstrated decreases in anxiety (Moran, 1996; Pasquali, 1990) and interruption in the cycle of stress (Pasquali, 1990). A study looking at nursing strategies that activate hopefulness in adolescents diagnosed with oncologic illness revealed that nurses who employed a light-hearted and playful attitude promoted feelings of hopefulness (Hunt, 1993). This study supports the positive influence humor has on feelings of hopefulness. Bellert (1989) reminds us that shared humor and laughter can enhance communication. "[Humor and laughter] allow the patient to consider alternative ways of looking at life, of exploring new coping skills, and of gaining control over health" (Bellert, 1989, p. 69). Bokun (1986) states that humor used as therapy when dealing with cancer patients offers nothing to lose but worries.

Kuiper, Martin, and Olinger (1993) performed a study looking at humor and cognitive appraisal of potentially stressful events using academic examinations. The study confirmed the theories that those with higher humor scores would be able to use humor effectively to distance themselves from stressful life events. Individuals who scored as high humor users were found to deal with stressful situations in a more direct fashion. The study also revealed that people with high humor scores tended to be less vulnerable to threats to their self-esteem than those with lower humor scores.

A study by Labott and Martin (1987) on the moderating effects of emotional weeping and humor on negative life events revealed that, in all but the male group who reported weeping frequently, those who used humor found that it helped to decrease the intensity of a negative experience. Martin and Lefcourt (1983) reported that, as negative life events increase, people using humor to cope report less mood disturbances than individuals who are less likely to use humor. Labott, Ahleman, Wolever, and Martin (1990) also discovered that using humor to cope was associated with more positive moods.

Two studies by Lefcourt, Davidson, Shepherd, Phillips, Prakachin, and Mills (1995) looked at ways in which humor could account for the stress-moderating effects found in other humor studies. The researchers looked at perspective-taking humor. Perspective-taking humor is defined as "a readiness to assume a remote and comic vision of ourselves" (Lefcourt et al., 1995, p. 387). Most of the subjects in these studies reported dysphoria after taking part in stress-producing, death-related activities. Those individuals who rated high in perspective-taking humor showed little change in affect. The studies also revealed that individuals who were able to understand and enjoy the cartoons used in the studies had positive emotional effects. Lefcourt

and colleagues (1995) concluded that people who can envision their lives from a remote perspective may be better able to think about catastrophic events without becoming excessively distressed. This study was conducted using humor as a means of coping with stressful events, indicating that humor may offer a means of reframing how we see ourselves in situations that are related to death.

It has been argued that laughter and crying are both cathartics — measures that can be used to release tension (Goodheart, 1994). Labott and Martin (1987) looked at the effects of crying and humor on stress modification. Crying did not prove to be a buffer against life stress in the college students who participated. Humor, on the other hand, did prove to buffer life stress in all categories except males categorized by high crying.

A study by Makinen, Suominen, and Lauri (2000) investigated the mechanisms that help adult asthma patients cope with their disease. They found that social support played a significant part in patients' ability to fight a sense of powerlessness. Ninety-one percent said that humor helped them cope with psychological self-care, whereas 80% said that positive thinking helped. On the humor scale, 49 people said they totally agreed that humor helped, 42 said they agreed that it helped, 9 were not sure, and only 1 said humor did not help. Of all the parameters this study researched regarding psychological self-care (positive thinking, finding time for self, exercise, actively pushing aside negative thinking, crying, and humor) the only parameter that no one checked as "totally disagree" was humor.

Concerns about coping strategies used by caregivers of pediatric patients led Wade, Borawski, Taylor, Drotar, Yeates, and Stancin (2001) to investigate the types of coping mechanisms used by parents of children who experienced traumatic brain injury (TBI) and children with orthopedic injuries. One of the strategies investigated was the use of humor. This study was the first to look at specific outcomes of caregiver and family coping during the initial year following pediatric injury. It was also the first to look at differences in the severity of injury, coping strategies, and caregiver and family outcomes. The study sample included 109 children with moderate-to-severe TBI and 80 children with orthopedic injuries that had no central nervous system insult. The parent most likely to take part in the study was the mother.

The study by Wade and colleagues. (2001) indicated that caregivers generally relied most on religion. Active coping, planning, and seeking of emotional support to deal with their child's injury followed. Humor and denial or disengagement were used less comonly. Immediately following the injury, parents whose children sustained orthopedic injuries were somewhat more likely to use humor than parents of children with TBI. This study found that the caregivers of children with TBI who used humor to cope soon after the injury had a significantly lower level of psychological symptoms at 12 months postinjury than did the caregivers in the orthopedic injury group.

Overall, emotion-focused coping strategies (of which humor was one of the mechanisms) were associated with better caregiver and family outcomes, whereas denial and disengagement were associated with more negative outcomes (Wade et al., 2001). The relationship between coping and caregiver response varied depending on the severity of the injury. This indicates that certain coping strategies may be influenced by the nature of the stressor. Of the coping mechanisms investigated, humor use reduced caregiver distress from 6 to 12 months after TBI, but it did not have the same effect following orthopedic injuries. This finding could be because orthopedic injuries are self-limiting, and TBI requires many different adjustments and remains a prevailing experience in the life of the child and family. It is possible that coming to terms with the multiple problems, or even joking about them, may let the caregiver cope more effectively with sequelae of the injury.

Humor has also been studied as a coping mechanism in cancer adjustment (Wikliniski, 1994; Johnson, 2002). Cancer patients report that humor was an important element in helping them deal with their illness. Laughter helps cancer patients escape from the fears of pain, disfigurement, and potential death. Humor helped patients connect with others who were important in their lives.

For example, Sally was diagnosed with breast cancer and was receiving chemotherapy. When she knew she was going to lose her hair, we sent her to her hairdresser. She said she wanted to have her head shaved. The first thing the hairdresser did was give her a Mohawk and they took pictures. This lightened the mood. The appointment had started out seriously, but when they took out the camera, they started to have fun. Soon after that day, when the stubble began to fall out, she thought it would be difficult for her and her girls to deal with. Once again, she decided to have some fun. She took out two of her leg shavers, got her two daughters, sat on a towel on the floor of the bathroom, and her daughters shaved her head. They all had a great time laughing and joking, and her daughters felt they were helping their mom with her cancer.

A news article in *USA Today* by Marilyn Elias (2003) discusses the possibility that happy people live longer than unhappy people. Elias quotes a study that reported that happy adults with heart disease are 20% more likely than unhappy adults with heart disease to live another 11 years. The reason for this difference in survival is not clear; however, researchers hypothesize that positive emotions do not trigger stress hormones which can make blood platelets thicker and thicken the blood.

Ongoing research by the Baltimore Longitudinal Study of Aging indicates that cheerful people complain less about chest pain. Also, unhappy people are more likely to isolate themselves, not take their medications as prescribed, and eat less healthy and are less likely to exercise than cheerful people. In other words, people who can find things to be joyful about are more likely to live fuller, happier, and longer lives. Humor is one way to put a new perspective on negative events in life, and it helps maintain a sense of happiness.

Humor can also be used to help people distance themselves from stressful situations. For example, Nazi prisoners used humor as a survival mechanism (Frankl, 1963; Henman, 2001). Henman's (2001) study of prisoners of the Vietnam war indicates the importance of humor as a stress-reduction method as well as a survival mechanism. In an online article about humor during the war with Iraq, Dr. Paul Wong (2003) states, "Humor also allows one to move from rigidity to openness, from despair to hope, and from fear to the celebration of life. With humor and laughter, we not only cope better, but also become healthier and happier."

DYING, DEATH, AND HUMOR

Dying

Some people think that humor has no place in the dying process. Alan Klein (1998) tried to dispel that myth in his book *Courage to Laugh* . He talked to people who were dying and people who were bereaved and compiled their stories about humor and coping. The result is a book that is filled with examples of how people can take charge of the dying process or the bereavement over loss of a loved one and use humor to lighten the grief or the pain of loss.

Part of the problem with exploring the use of humor during the care of the terminally ill involves American culture's avoidance of and discomfort with death. Death is considered a solemn affair. However, if a person is dying, does he or she really want to be sad and solemn all the time? What about the belief that life is to be lived until death? Yes, pain and deterioration may occur during the dying

process; however, humor can still be employed to try to offer a period of relief.

Hospice nurses Graham and Cates (cited in Herth, 1995) suggest that humor provides care for the whole person, something that is now known to be important in healthcare. Humor encourages expression of a range of emotions, helps facilitate coping with pain and loss, and helps provide a way of framing life even if life is limited (Herth, 1995). Branum (1990, cited in Herth, 1995) believes "that humor provides a momentary escape into a place of freedom and power" (p. 219). This can be a wonderful gift to someone who has a sense of powerlessness.

Herth (1995) conducted a study that involved 14 terminally ill adults. Many of them expressed that sharing something positive made them feel like "a real person again" (Herth, 1995, p. 220). Most expressed a sentiment that has also been expressed by cancer patients: Humor allowed them to see things in a more positive manner and put a new light on their situations. Several of the patients felt that the constant seriousness of their present situation made them feel isolated "and as if they were already dead" (Herth, 1995, p. 220). The participants felt that humor enhanced and enriched their lives even though their time on earth was limited.

Because dying is serious business, it might be up to the nurse to send signals that tell the patient that it is okay to laugh. Once people sense that humor is okay, they are more likely to share and bring forth their own humor potential. When dealing with the dying, it is important to allow room for all ranges of emotion; too much humor, like too much crying, can wear on the patient.

Death and Bereavement

Bereavement is a painful process for mourners. Mourning saps energy and causes feelings of depression and possibly, fear. Humor can offer some relief to the pain of grief and can decrease depression and improve energy levels. For some, the best way to understand the benefits of laughter is through stories of those who have used humor to cope. Herth (1995) tells one such story about a funeral she attended for a 68-year-old gentleman she had cared for through a hospice program:

> This particular gentleman had a great sense of humor and had always been the "life of a party." Prior to entering the sanctuary of the church, the family, close friends, and myself were secluded in a room just off to the side. The silence in the room was deafening. The minister asked if anyone wanted to ask or say anything before we went into the church. Remembering his joy for living, I asked if anyone could think of specific times they had spent with him that brought a sense of delight and joy to the heart that we could share before entering the sanctuary. One of the family members shared a humorous, joyful time they had together, and immediately other members shared similar experiences. The family and friends recognized that this gentleman would want his funeral to be a celebration of his life and his joy for living. . . . Several weeks later, several family members and friends told me how much it had meant to share the joyous moments at the funeral, and how important this was to them as they were working through the grieving process. (p. 222-223)

Humor is one way members of bereavement groups can connect with one another and share their respective grief. During the seventh meeting of an 8-week bereavement group, a female member shared that friends of hers were taking her to a club that has male strippers. They had decided it was time for her to "let go and cut up" a little. Another member of the group, an elderly gentleman who had lost his wife of 62 years, perked up as she was talking. Someone started teasing her about putting money in the dancer's G-string. Suddenly, this gen-

tleman, who was usually very quiet, said, "Would you put money in my G-string if I danced for you?" Everyone started to laugh. The next week, at the final meeting, which consisted of a pizza dinner, the participants were still laughing and teasing both of them about the week before. The gentleman who had been so depressed and quiet was laughing and participating in the fun. The gentleman's response was a good indication of the beginning of a healing process. It was wonderful to see the difference a little bit of humor made in the lives of the woman and the older gentleman as well as the other participants.

SUMMARY

The psychosocial aspects of humor are important elements in coping with life stress and relationship formation. Humor helps people connect with one another. It is a great communicator. It also helps put life events into perspective. Studies by Frecknall (1994) and Beck (1997) demonstrate the use of humor as a form of connection between people. The participants in Bippus's (2000) study claimed that humor was comforting during stressful situations. Lippert's (2001) study demonstrates that humor is essential to the relationships that develop between nurses and long-term care residents. These studies, and others, indicate the importance of using humor to build relationships.

Positive relationships are an important part of patient care. Whether the patient is dealing with a non-terminal illness, or at the last stages of the life process, humor offers an outlet for stress and builds relationships between the nurse and the patient. Klein (1998) says that "humor helps us keep our balance when life throws us a curve ball" (p. 4). Using humor in the healthcare setting may help patients "keep their balance."

EXAM QUESTIONS

CHAPTER 4
Questions 28-36

28. Humor is important in social situations because it

    a. can help hide a person's fears.

    b. helps a person become more popular.

    c. helps a person breathe better when stress occurs.

    d. improves communication by dissolving barriers.

29. When examining gender and social hierarchy in humor, studies have shown

    a. members of a group with higher status tell more jokes.

    b. members of a group with lower status tell more jokes.

    c. women tell more jokes than men.

    d. men laugh at jokes more than women.

30. When nurses use humor judiciously with patients it

    a. helps increase rapport between the nurse and patient.

    b. lets the patient know that the nurse is in charge.

    c. tells the patient that everything will be all right.

    d. increases the game of pretend so patients feel less stress.

31. Using humor in serious situations

    a. is always appropriate in any situation.

    b. is never appropriate in any situation.

    c. might be helpful if used carefully.

    d. is always hurtful to the person involved in the situation.

32. A patient says to his nurse, "The doctor says my disease is terminal. I guess I better cash in my bonds," and starts to laugh. The best action by the nurse is to

    a. laugh with the patient and then leave.

    b. ask an open-ended question to assess level of distress.

    c. ask the patient if he would like to speak to a social worker.

    d. ask the patient if he would like something from the humor cart.

33. With regard to personal advertisements, it has been noted that

    a. men tend to want women who have a sense of humor.

    b. women look for men who have a sense of humor.

    c. men want women who will make them laugh.

    d. women are not interested in a sense of humor.

34. The use of humor with people who are dying

    a. is inappropriate and hurtful.

    b. is better for the nurse than the patient.

    c. encourages denial of death.

    d. is considered life-enhancing.

35. One of the most significant advantages to the use of humor in stressful situations is that it

    a. resolves the problem.

    b. prevents mood swings.

    c. can change a person's perspective.

    d. can lead to laughter.

36. The use of humor in a bereavement group

    a. helps members connect/share their grief.

    b. prevents us from coping with a death.

    c. avoids telling stories of the deceased.

    d. increases our anxiety about death.

CHAPTER 5

DEVELOPMENT OF HUMOR APPRECIATION

CHAPTER OBJECTIVE

After completing this chapter, the reader will be able to describe how humor develops from infancy to adulthood.

LEARNING OBJECTIVES

After studying this chapter, the reader will be able to

1. describe the emergence of humor in children.

2. identify how children's understanding and response to humor develops as children age.

3. describe what children consider funny at different ages.

4. contrast adolescent humor to the humor of those under age 12.

5. differentiate between children's and adults' humor.

INTRODUCTION

Children and adults appreciate humor differently. Humor does not just happen; it is a product of development. Children do not laugh at things that they do not have the capacity to understand. Much humor comes from incongruity. Because children do not have the experience that develops throughout life, they do not have the capacity to see incongruity with the same perspective as adults. This generally makes a child's sense of humor more limited than an adult's. As the child ages, the ability to appreciate and understand humor changes. This chapter explores the development of humor from childhood to adulthood.

THE EARLY YEARS: INFANCY TO AGE 2

It has been said that children laugh 400 times a day. Although there is no scientific research to back up that statistic, researchers do know that children appear to laugh far more than adults do. Humor development begins at a very early age. The beginning evidence of a sense of humor can be seen as early as the third or fourth month of age (Herzog, 2004). Mimicking parents is an important function in humor development because that is how children learn (Herzog, 2004). At this age, the expression of humor may come in the form of a smile or laughter. A smile is usually an indication of pleasure. It is also a means of communication. Ziv (1984) describes the smile as the "first form of positive communication" (p. 27). In infancy, a smile communicates the message "I feel good" (Ziv, 1984). Babies typically smile by age 3 months. People used to believe that infant smiles were a response to gas; however, they are now believed to be a response to fluctuations in a baby's level of arousal (Clark, 2002). By 6-weeks-old, most babies grin in response to a grinning face. A laughter response can be seen in children as young as age 3 months. One can see this response when a baby is tickled, kissed on the abdomen, or bounced (Clark, 2002).

Ziv (1984) states that until 8 weeks of age, the social smile occurs with recognition of human faces and voices in general. He further states that after 8 weeks of age, a baby's smile appears to be more selective, expressing recognition of a mother or father. An infant's smile appears to play an important part in the dialogue between parent and baby. The selective smile occurs at the time an infant moves from passivity to directed activity in other areas of life (Holland, 1982). By age 3 months, infants begin to respond to humorous events through nonreflexive laughter (Reddy, Williams, & Vaughan, 2002). In other words, an infant may respond with laughter or a smile to such phrases as "I'm going to get you," as well as to the physical stimulation of tickling or bouncing. The physical stimulation response results in laughter because it gives the immature nervous system a mild and pleasant jolt (Clark, 2002).

An interesting experiment noted that infants under the age of 8 months need to see the combination of forehead, nose, and two eyes to respond with a smile (Holland, 1982). A child will smile at a nodding Halloween mask that contains the proper features; however, he or she will not smile at the profile of a human face. As the infant ages, smiling only if the combination of forehead, nose and eyes are visible will begin to change and the child will smile a smile that conveys recognition for loved adults. While the child will smile at adults he or she recognizes, the response to strangers may result in expressions of anxiety

One of the prerequisites for a sense of humor is the ability to recognize incongruences. A baby typically starts to demonstrate this ability between ages 6 and 9 months (Clark, 2002). Babies may respond to such behaviors as oinking like a pig or making "horse lips." Around age 7 months, babies begin to understand that objects are still there even if they

cannot be seen; therefore, peekaboo and pop-up toys become funny. Playing "I'm going to get you" or kissing the baby's abdomen becomes even funnier because the baby is now able to anticipate what is coming.

An infant responds to a new stimulus with curiosity and attempts to manipulate the stimulus by touching or otherwise coming in contact with it. This behavior reflects an effort to understand and master the environment. An infant seems to respond with a smile to a new stimulus that has similarities with something the child finds familiar (Ziv, 1984), especially once they are sure that the stimulus is not harmful. If the stimulus is then presented on a continuous basis, the infant appears to become tired or bored with the effort to elicit a smile, and the smile disappears. This response may be a way of expressing the enjoyment of discovery and a sense of victory in problem solving.

As children continue to develop, they begin to recognize and understand events that are incongruent. By age 11 or 12 months, infants laugh at funny faces and sounds or funny events, such as a person waddling like a duck or an adult sucking from a baby bottle (Reddy et al., 2002). By age 10 months, many children have started to initiate humor and begin laughing even before the end of a humorous event.

Humor development can be understood by looking at Piaget's developmental tasks. The first task is sensorimotor, which occurs from birth to age 2 years. During this stage, the child begins to understand that objects continue to exist even when they cannot be touched, seen, or heard. They also begin to understand that things do not just happen. They are caused by something or someone. As children age, they begin to realize that they can affect events by behaving in certain ways. Reddy et al. (2002) note that children begin to recognize that they can cause others to laugh by clowning and teasing. Piaget mentions that one of his daughters at 1½ years of age pretended to eat with no food in front of her. His second daughter, at about the same age, pretended to brush her teeth with her finger as if it were a toothbrush. These behaviors were accompanied by a smile and laughter (Newman & Newman, 1999).

AGES 2 TO 7

Piaget's preoperational thought developmental stage occurs approximately between ages 2 and 7. During this stage, a child has increased language skills and can recognize differences in thought from action (Howe, 1993). Children who have reached the preoperational stage and have an image-based representational capacity have the ability to find humor in acting on one object as if it were another object (Martin, 1989)—for example, a child who laughs at a picture of a hippopotamus trying to get on a pair of pants. After all, hippopotamuses don't wear pants, people do.

One function of humor is to release tension (Klein, 1992). At age 2, children begin to experience many conflict situations. They start learning that their views and goals are often not shared by the adults in their lives. The use of humorous situations presented in books or cartoons appears to help them learn that difficult problems can be resolved in constructive ways.

Two-year-olds typically like stories based on experiences that they find physically challenging, such as walking, running, dressing, undressing, and bathing themselves (Klein, 1992). Being able to laugh at the silly mistakes depicted in storybooks helps children realize that they can or have developed mastery over some of these behaviors. Humor helps children explore and cope with issues that can be a source of anxiety, which is one reason why most preschool and kindergarten children laugh at potty humor (Barasch, 1999). Humor helps learning because it motivates, arouses, and stimulates the child's cognitive processes (Klein, 1992; McGhee, 1989). Flatter (n.d.) states that 2- and 3-year-olds

are prone to copycat humor, which is part of a pattern of modeling behaviors.

During the preschool years, children attempt to master spoken language. This attempt can make nonsense words a source of enjoyment (Barasch, 1999). Children learning to use language sometimes deliberately use a wrong word as they play with their own and others' reactions to language. After all, one way to learn a new skill is to play with it. Children may distort words, make up words, or cause nonsense words to rhyme and demonstrate joy in their ability to make something seem funny. Although they have not yet figured out what makes a joke funny, they begin to tell jokes and riddles.

One word of caution when working with preschoolers: there may be a very fine line between what is funny and what is frightening to them (Flatter, n.d.). A clown wearing exaggerated face paint and a bright orange wig might elicit reactions of fear rather than amusement. Activities that are too out of the ordinary or playacting that goes on too long may cause feelings of anxiety.

Kindergarten children find almost everything funny (Howe, 1993). This age-group is especially fond of clowns, funny stories about animals and people, and bathroom humor. Bathroom humor can be as simple as mentioning the word "underwear." Kindergartners' humor seems to reflect their silliness and lack of "cognitive sophistication" (Howe, 1993).

To investigate the ability of young children to understand and appreciate cognitively oriented humor, Klein (1995) studied the relationship between humor comprehension and three forms of humor appreciation. The results of this study indicate that children between 5 and 6 years old are able to describe or explain joking relationships, demonstrating comprehension of intended humor.

Bariaud (1989) notes that children between ages 3 and 5 find humor in things that represent incongruity in appearances, such as a cow taking a bath and washing himself with a scrub brush. At approximately age 6, a change in joking style takes place. Prior to age 6, children seem to enjoy their own inventions of humor, and the humor tends to be spontaneous, original, and relatively crude (Bariaud, 1989). At age 6 children begin to show an interest in ready-made jokes. This interest continues to develop between ages 7 and 10 (Bariaud, 1989).

At age 7, a change in humor appreciation occurs (Bariaud, 1989). Seven-year-olds may respond in a serious manner to riddles that 1 year earlier would have caused laughter (Bariaud, 1989). Watching 7-year-olds try to decipher a cartoon so that the incongruity in it made sense led Bariaud (1989) to conclude that children of this age have not mastered the "convention according to which such cartoons purposefully distort things in order to be funny" (p. 38). In this study using cartoons, Bariaud (1989) found that 7-year-olds would explain that the cartoon could not be funny because "it can't be like that" (p. 38). Not all 7-year-olds responded in this manner, but a significant number did. Howe (1993) notes that this age-group find cartoons, clowns, and riddles enjoyable. They tend to like patterns of riddles, like elephant or knock-knock jokes, and may tell them for weeks. They delight in trying to outwit adults with the riddles (Barasch, 1999; Howe, 1993).

Joking is a way of connecting with others. Adults use humor in social situations to improve relationships. Children around 6 and 7 years old begin to realize that humor can help them gain acceptance, approval or, if nothing else, someone's attention (Barasch, 1999).

Adults are not the only ones who use humor to cope with fears and anxieties. Children also find that humor helps them cope with these emotions. As children start exploring the outside world, humor works to defuse some of the anxiety they experience (Barasch, 1999). Jokes that make fun of others, such as those with disabilities, may be a way for children to deal with their own fears of being injured, disabled, or somehow different from others. Tyson (n.d.) cautions that laughter may be a way of soothing anxiety,

but it might not be connected with humor. As an example, a child may laugh when another child trips or something angers the teacher. This laughter might be a way of distancing themselves from the fears aroused by an uncomfortable situation.

AGES 7 TO 12

According to Piaget, children ages 7 to 12 are in the concrete operational stage. Howe (1993) notes that third-grade children begin to demonstrate less fear of authority, and this seems to lead to teachers becoming a source of humor. A study by Socha (1994) investigated the use of prosocial and antisocial humor. Antisocial humor refers to the type of humor that pokes fun at different people. It can be hurtful to an individual or a group. He discovered that children up to fourth grade tended to use more prosocial humor than antisocial humor. If antisocial behavior was used, it was usually used by boys and aimed at other children. Up until eighth grade, children were more likely to use humor that had some decorum when communicating with teachers. The eighth grade children who demonstrated less polite humor, such as teasing the teacher about hair loss, seemed to be comfortable with the teacher they were teasing.

Socha (1994) found a significant change from prosocial to antisocial joke telling in the fourth grade. This change was significantly greater for boys than for girls. The boys' behavior showed an increased tendency to make fun of others. Girls also tended to make fun of others, but not to the same extent as did the boys.

Howe (1993) states that fourth graders tend to use humor that revolves around their peers, with increased emphasis on the opposite sex and friends' mistakes. They do not see other students getting in trouble as funny, as is the tendency of those in third grade. A study by Shade (1991) found that fourth-grade children enjoyed jokes and riddles over puns and satire. This is probably indicative of their cognitive level, which is not developed enough to enjoy puns and satire. Children of this age still take comments very literally (Howe, 1993; Shade, 1991).

By fifth grade, children begin to show a decrease in slapstick humor and an increase in more social humor. According to Howe (1993), the humor found in others making mistakes greatly increases among this age-group. This behavior was noticed in fourth graders by Socha (1994).

By fourth or fifth grade, there is a noticeable difference between boys' humor and girls' humor. Around age 10, boys tend to tell jokes that are sexual or physically violent. Girls at the same age like humor that is more verbally aggressive rather than physically violent. They tend to tease each other about boyfriends and "act like caricatures of the vamps they see on television soap operas." Despite the differences, jokes are an indirect way for each group to deal with the issues they are most concerned about, such as their sexuality (Kutner, n.d.).

Sixth-grade humor shows a continued increase in the use of social humor. Howe (1993) notes that mistakes made by others, especially peers, top the list of things that are funny. Cognitive understanding improves in this age-group and incongruities are better understood. Crude behavior and grossness is likely to be seen as humorous, especially by boys. Boys also tend to find body noises funny, just as they did in first grade (Howe, 1993).

PREADOLESCENCE AND ADOLESCENCE

Around the age of 12, children move into Piaget's fourth stage: formal operational thought. By this age, children can think hypothetically. Although it is a gradual development, the ability to think abstractly becomes more fully developed, allowing the child to think of a number of scenarios when asked how things might be different. At this age, children begin to actively use humor for coping with stressful life events (Fuhr,

2002). They also begin to make jokes about their situation. For example, a 12-year-old deliberately uses humor to deal with an upcoming heart transplant (Dowling, 2002).

Fuhr (2002) studied the form and function of humor in children ages 12 to 16 from Copenhagen. He studied students in two different schools to see if there was a difference between humor use and appreciation in students from the country versus students from a town. Fuhr's study indicated that some types of jokes were preferred more by one group than another. The differences appeared to be connected with life situations. This study confirms Kutner's (n.d.) comment that children's humor seems to be connected to the developmental tasks with which they are struggling. The three areas that had notable differences were: (1) "plans for the future," which was of higher interest to town children; (2) "boyfriends or girlfriends," which was also of higher interest in children from town, and (3) "other," which was of higher interest to children from the country (Fuhr, 2002).

Sex-related jokes were found to have a high level of interest for 12- to 13-year-olds in Fuhr's 2002 study. Sex was the most important theme for 12-year-olds in particular. Sex was more important for boys than for girls.

With increased age, the use of coping humor increased (Fuhr, 2002). This is believed to be due to increased experiences and the witnessing of others using humor to cope.

Very few studies explore the development of the type of humor enjoyed in adolescence. What we do know is that, as children develop, gain experience, and synthesize information, their appreciation and understanding of humor changes and becomes more adultlike. Klause (1987) notes that teens appear to enjoy puns. This enjoyment of puns decreases as individuals move into adulthood. However, the cognitive process of formulating the pun seems to bring enjoyment to the one who designs it (Klause, 1987).

ADULTHOOD

As with other areas of human development, when a person reaches adulthood, humor development seems to stop. However, humor responses and usage continue to develop and change as a person continues to age. The research on how humor appreciation of adults changes over time is limited (Ruch, McGhee, Hehl, 1990), although a few studies have explored how older adults respond to humor in different situations. Listed below are descriptions of two examples of humor that are commonly seen in adults.

McGhee, Ruch, and Hehl (cited in Ruch et al., 1990) suggest a model of humor development in adulthood. According to this model, there is a strong link between age, differences in personality variables such as intolerance of ambiguity and sensation seeking, and appreciation of humorous materials such as cartoons and jokes. Ruch et al. (1990) report that studies demonstrate that more- conservative people find "incongruity-resolution humor funnier and less aversive than do more liberal individuals"

Incongruity-resolution humor occurs when a joke begins with an incongruity which is then fully resolved by the end of the joke. One example of this is the following:

What is grey, has four legs, and a trunk?
A mouse on vacation.

Nonsense humor has a surprise punch line, but there is either no resolution, a partial resolution, or there may be a new absurdity or incongruity. Puns and limericks are examples of nonsense humor. The following limerick is an example of nonsense humor:

There was a young man of St. Kitts,
Who was very much troubled with fits,
The eclipse of the moon
Threw him into a swoon,
Then he tumbled and broke into bits.

(p. 348). The opposite is true of nonsense humor. Individuals who have an increased intolerance to ambiguity appreciate incongruity-resolution humor more than nonsense humor. This finding is consistent with the view that these personality dimensions are most likely to dislike or avoid novel, complex, incongruous, or ambiguous events that leave a person in a state of high subjective uncertainty.

Cross-sectional studies demonstrate age differences in the personality dimensions of conservatism, sensation seeking, and intolerance of ambiguity (Ruch et al., 1990). Much of the data indicates that sensation seeking peaks in the late teens or early 20s and then decreases with age. Conservatism commonly begins to appear in the late 20s and increases until past age 60.

Ruch et al. conducted a cross-sectional study of 4,292 subjects to test the McGhee, Ruch, and Hehl model. The study included 3,057 males ages 14 to 66 and 1,235 females ages 14 to 54. The researchers recognized that cohort differences might exist among the subjects, in that the older adults might always have been more conservative and less sensation seeking than the younger adults. The researchers were looking to discover if appreciation of incongruity-resolution humor increased with age, beginning in the late 20s or early 30s, and if appreciation of nonsense humor changed with a progressive drop after age 30.

The researchers found that their results were relatively consistent with the McGhee, Ruch, Hehl model. They also found a few areas of interest. First, 14- to 16-year-olds demonstrated relatively high incongruity-resolution scores. Then, nonsense humor scales increased until the late 20s, when the incongruity-resolution scores began to gradually increase. Those individuals in their 40s showed a sharp increase in incongruity-resolution humor appreciation. This was consistent with the increase in conservatism.

All ages younger than the 29 to 31 age-group, (except the 14- to 16-year-olds, who found incongruity-resolution humor funnier than nonsense humor), judged the two humor structures comparably funny (Ruch et al., 1990). This pattern began to change with an increase in incongruity-resolution humor appreciation. One drawback of this study is that it was cross-sectional and not longitudinal, so the changes found might reflect age-group differences rather than changes that occur as people age. A longitudinal study following the same group of adults over time would be more likely to answer the question of how humor might change as people age.

A recently reported study from Baycrest Centre for Geriatric Care (2003) in Toronto found that humor appreciation does not change with age. However, this study found that comprehension of complex forms of humor does diminish with age. The study was conducted using 20 healthy older adults whose average age was 73 and 17 healthy younger adults whose average age was 28. To understand the results, it is helpful to understand the tasks requested of the participants.

The participants were asked to complete three separate humor tests: differentiating humorous statements from neutral statements, joke and story completion, and nonverbal cartoon appreciation. The first test looked at humor appreciation. It consisted of 21 humorous and 7 neutral statements. Examples of humorous statements included a sign in a tailor shop that read, "Please have a fit upstairs," and a sign in a hotel that read, "Guests are invited to take advantage of the chambermaid" (Baycrest Centre for Geriatric Care, 2003, ¶10). One of the neutral statements was a sign in a hotel that read, "Visitors are requested to turn off the lights when they leave the room."

The second test consisted of having the participants choose the correct punch lines for 16 incomplete joke stems. Only one of the four endings offered was the correct humorous punch line. The third test consisted of 10 different cartoon drawings. Each cartoon had a series of four similar drawings, but only one had a funny detail. Participants were asked to choose the funny version.

This study found that older adults did just as well as the younger participants on the first test. However, the older adults made significant mistakes on the two more cognitively challenging tests. The difficulty in comprehending more complex forms of humor may be related to age-related changes in the frontal lobes. Biological evidence suggests that frontal lobe functions may be the first to decline with age (Baycrest Centre for Geriatric Care, 2003). Despite their difficulty comprehending more complex humor, the older participants reacted appropriately with a smile or laugh when they did understand the humor. This suggests that the humor processing related to other regions in the brain remains intact.

The researchers of this study caution that the study was just preliminary. Overinterpretation of the results needs to be avoided. Limitations of the study include small sample size and a lack of investigation of cohort differences in the type of humor preferred, social setting, or health — all of which contribute to our response to humorous situations.

Table 5-1 summarizes the developmental stages of humor by age, as noted by the above studies.

SUMMARY

The development of humor from childhood to adulthood has received attention from the scientific community. One of the first people to research the development of humor in children was Paul McGhee. Since then, others have researched development of humor from different perspectives, such as Fuhr's research into the use of coping humor in children ages 12 to 16. The understanding of humorous material changes as children develop cognitively. This development of humor continues into adulthood, as the events that trigger a humor response take on different meanings. Research suggests that older adults do not lose their ability to appreciate humor, but changes in the frontal lobe can lead to diminished ability to understand complex humor.

TABLE 5-1: HUMOR DEVELOPMENT REVIEW (1 OF 2)	
Cognitive Stage and Age	**Developmental Behaviors**
Sensorimotor 6 weeks	• Baby grins at a grinning face. • Baby smiles in recognition of human faces and voices.
8 weeks	• Baby becomes more selective, grinning only at mother or father. • Baby attempts a type of dialogue with parents.
3 months	• Baby begins to smile or laugh at certain phrases, tickling, or bouncing.
6 to 9 months	• Baby begins to recognize incongruences. • Baby may smile or laugh at pig sounds or funny faces.
Around 7 months	• Peekaboo and pop-up toys become funny. • Baby begins to anticipate reactions, so playing "I'm going to get you" or kissing the abdomen becomes funnier.
8 months and younger	• The combination of forehead, nose, and eyes are needed for smile response.
8 months and older	• Combination of facial feature response decreases, and the child smiles at recognition of loved adults.
10 months	• Child may initiate humor.
11 or 12 months	• Child laughs at funny faces, sounds, or a person making animal movements such as waddling like a duck.
Preoperational 2 to 5 years	• Child is prone to copy-cat humor (ages 2 to 3). • Increased language skills and recognition of differences between thought and action can lead to the ability to find humor in pictures or stories of incongruent behavior. • Child laughs at silly mistakes depicted in books. • Child begins to understand that humor can be used to help cope with new and difficult situations. • Child likes to experiment with new words and sounds and uses nonsense words to make humor. • Child demonstrates joy in making things seem funny. • Child begins to tell jokes and riddles. • Things that are outrageous, such as clowns with exaggerated face paint and bright orange wigs, might cause fear rather than amusement.
5 to 6 years	• Child finds almost everything funny. • Child laughs at insults, practical jokes, and accidents that happen to others. • Child is fond of clowns and funny stories. • Child likes bathroom humor. • Child is able to explain joking relationships. • Child begins to show an interest in ready-made jokes.

TABLE 5-1: HUMOR DEVELOPMENT REVIEW (2 OF 2)

Concrete Operational 7 years	• Child seems to become more serious. • Humor is more reality based. • Child likes cartoon, riddles, and clowns. • Child likes to try to outwit adults with riddles.
7 to 12 years	• Child begins to demonstrate less fear of authority, making teachers a source of humor. • Child tends to use mainly prosocial humor (between ages 7 and 9). • Child laughs at reality-oriented, more-complex riddles that fit into the child's understanding of the world. • Child exhibits an increase in antisocial humor and an increase in making fun of others (9-year-olds). • Child enjoys jokes and riddles over puns and satire. • Child begins to move from slapstick humor to more social humor (10-year-olds). • Boys' humor differs from girls' humor (9- and 10-year-olds). • Child demonstrates increased use of social humor (11- and 12-year-olds). • Child still sees mistakes by others as funny. • Boys tend to find body noises funny, similar to first grade enjoyment.
Formal Operational 12 years	• Gradual ability to think abstractly leads to increased use of humor as a coping mechanism. • Child exhibits increased enjoyment of sexual jokes, especially with boys.
Adolescence	• Use of coping humor increases. • Adolescent still enjoys puns. • Adolescent has a high incongruity-resolution score (14- to 16-year-olds).
Adulthood	• Conservative individuals appreciate incongruity-resolution humor. • Enjoyment of nonsense humor increases with age.
Older Adulthood	• Humor appreciation does not change with age. • Understanding of complex humor decreases.

Data for this table was accumulated from Barasch, 1999; Bariaud, 1989; Clark, 2002; Herzog, 2004; McGhee, 1989; Reddy, Williams, Vaughan, 2002; Ruch, McGhee, & Hehl, 1990; Socha, 1994; and Ziv, 1984.

EXAM QUESTIONS

CHAPTER 5
Questions 37-45

37. Babies become more selective in their smiling responses to others at age

    a. 3 weeks.
    b. 8 weeks.
    c. 3 months.
    d. 8 months.

38. According to Holland's experiment, infants younger than age 8 months smile in response to

    a. the profile of a human face.
    b. a mask of a one-eyed monster.
    c. recognition of incongruence.
    d. a view of a forehead, two eyes, and a nose.

39. An example of humor that requires a child to recognize incongruence is

    a. oinking like a pig.
    b. saying "I'm going to get you."
    c. playing peekaboo.
    d. tickling.

40. According to Flatter, the use of humorous situations in cartoons and storybooks allows the 2- to 3-year-olds to

    a. learn and repeat ready-made jokes.
    b. use copycat behavior to model behavior.
    c. change feelings by increasing anxiety.
    d. develop a sense of incongruence.

41. Because of their cognitive level, children around the age of 7

    a. have fun experimenting with new words and sounds.
    b. enjoy nonsense humor.
    c. like humor that is more reality based.
    d. laugh at silly mistakes depicted in books.

42. The use of sexual humor is more prominent with boys who are age

    a. 2.
    b. 4.
    c. 8.
    d. 12.

43. Adolescent humor differs from humor for children under age 12. In adolescent humor

    a. incongruencies are not well understood.
    b. sex related jokes and puns are less prevalent.
    c. they are more likely to use humor to cope.
    d. spontaneous and original jokes are common.

44. Incongruity-resolution humor is commonly seen in adults. This type of humor

    a. begins with absurdity and ends with a resolution.

    b. begins with a resolution and ends with absurdity.

    c. begins with absurdity and ends with a partial resolution.

    d. begins with absurdity and has a nonsensical ending.

45. As adults increase in conservatism, their appreciation of humor becomes more

    a. sexually oriented.

    b. nonsense oriented.

    c. incongruity-resolution oriented.

    d. bathroom-humor oriented.

CHAPTER 6

USING HUMOR IN THE HEALTHCARE SETTING

CHAPTER OBJECTIVES

After completing this chapter, the reader will be able to explain how humor can be used in the healthcare setting to benefit nurses and their patients.

LEARNING OBJECTIVES

After studying this chapter, the reader will be able to

1. describe the three roles of humor in healthcare as defined by Buxman.

2. discuss the importance of humor as a prevention for burnout.

3. describe how nurses use humor to connect with their patients.

4. discuss the importance of incorporating humor into patient care.

5. articulate the process of taking a humor assessment.

6. recognize the differences between helpful and hurtful humor.

INTRODUCTION

Humor is an important component for helping to maintain health. This fact has been demonstrated in research as well as in the personal experiences of most individuals. Through the years, nurses have been cautioned that humor may not be appropriate when someone is feeling ill or dealing with life-threatening situations. However, even patients who are dying appreciate the use of humor (Herth, 1995). Not only is humor an important tool to use with patients, but it is also an important tool for nurses to use to deal with the tensions and stress of nursing. This chapter answers questions concerning appropriate use of humor. It also discusses the way in which nurses use and discuss humor with their patients and each other and as a method for decreasing the potential for burnout.

USING HUMOR TO SURVIVE NURSING

In this era of decreasing staff and increasing workload, how would nurses survive without humor? For example, consider the following scenario. You have seven acutely ill patients, a doctor is screaming for assistance with a procedure, a patient is in pain and constantly on her light, and down the hall a patient with dementia is yelling, "Help me, God. Oh please, help me, God." What do you do? Screaming is out, although that might be exactly what you feel like doing. What would happen if you took one moment, got on the intercom to the room of the patient with dementia, and said, "This is God. Now go to sleep." That happened one night at a small, rural hospital in southeast Arizona. The patient, who had barely slept since she arrived at the hospital, fell asleep and slept the rest of the evening.

Robinson (1991) notes that "the health professional's need for humor is as great as that of the client" (p. 73). Stressors arise daily in the healthcare setting. Nurses must choose how they respond to those stressors. There are many ways to deal with the stress of work. Humor is just one of them; however, the other options may be unacceptable in a healthcare setting. For example, nurses have no time for meditation or relaxation exercises, and yelling or crying is viewed as unprofessional. Humor can be helpful, even if the nurse just keeps the "joke" to herself. However, shared humor helps diffuse the situation even more.

Buxman (1998) describes three main functions of humor in the healthcare settings. These functions are: psychological, social, and communication.

Psychological

Humor releases tension and gives the user a different perspective on his or her situation. The release of tension can increase creativity and leads to "perceptual flexibility" that can help increase a nurse's sense of control. One way of doing this is to negatively overemphasize the event and look for the lunacy in the situation by asking, "How can this be worse?" For example, it is 6:30 p.m., and a nurse who has only a half hour before the end of a 12-hour shift receives three new admissions. The nurse could say to herself, "How can this be worse?" The nurse might realize that one of the assigned patients could code. He or she then thinks, "How can this be worse?" The code response team is busy with another code. The nurse would then continue to find more things that might go wrong. Doing this might help put the situation in better perspective.

Social

The sharing of amusement creates a bond. It also helps to establish an equal relationship and decreases the sense of perceived hierarchy, even if for only a moment. It is difficult to remain angry or upset at someone with whom you have shared humor.

Communication

Humor allows a person to express concern, fear, or anger in a jestful manner, thus being able to "save face" if the recipient of the message does not respond kindly. The person making the comment can say, "I was only joking." If a patient makes this comment, the nurse can look beyond the patient's words for an underlying emotion or meaning. If the patient is fearful or anxious, the nurse can devise an intervention to help the patient deal with the situation.

Effective use of humor can also help prevent the ever present possibility of burnout. Healthcare providers deal with the reality of illness, suffering, and death on a daily basis. Compassion and caring can leave a healthcare provider vulnerable to feelings of sympathy. Sympathy causes a person to feel another person's pain, and can leave a healthcare provider vulnerable to feelings of fear, anxiety, anger, or depression. Of all healthcare providers, nurses and nursing aides have the closest relationships with the individuals who need care. Humor works as a tool to allow the care provider a more detached perspective. As Christina Maslach (1982, cited in Wooten, 1996) states, "Sometimes things are so frustrating that to keep from crying, you laugh at a situation that may not be funny. You laugh but in your heart you know what's really happening. Nevertheless, you do it because your own needs are important. We're all human beings and have to be ourselves" (pg. 19).

One major factor in burnout is a sense of powerlessness. This sensation can leave a person feeling frustrated, angry, or hopeless. Some people give into that feeling and leave the profession as a means of emotional protection. Others are more resilient and experience less burnout. Resilient individuals are able to withstand the strains of life's stressors and bounce back from adversity by using coping methods such as humor. Humor helped Vietnam prisoners of war survive the rigors of torture and abuse without developing overwhelming posttraumatic stress disorder (Henman, 2001). Therefore, it should be helpful to nurses for the prevention of caregiver burnout.

One type of humor that commonly develops during times of high stress is gallows, or black, humor. Robinson (1991) notes, "Black humor is a defense against the horror, against whatever it is we fear, and is a way to master it and give us a sense of control by laughing at it" (p. 81). For healthcare staff, humor is a way of distancing oneself from the patient or the situation. Gallows humor allows the care provider to continue giving compassionate care because it releases tension. Robinson (1991) notes that joking among staff members does not interfere with their ability to care. In fact, it actually adds to the quality of performance because of the reduced perceived emotional stress (Robinson, 1991). One caution is needed, however. Gallows humor must be used judiciously. It can be hurtful if the wrong person overhears it.

Playing jokes on each other is one way nursing staff can use humor to alleviate stress. Here are two examples of practical jokes:

- In one hospital the nurses on the day shift would sometimes make an old woman out of pillows in an empty bed for the night nurse, with all the appropriate papers in a file (Astedt-Kurki & Isola, 2001).

- One of the LPNs came into the staff development office where Annie was being cleaned after a CPR class. She took Annie and carefully placed her on the toilet seat in the private bath of the office. The next person to enter the bathroom was the nursing director. The nursing director immediately turned around and said to the LPN, "Ms. P, you're at it again," at which point those in the office started laughing (personal experience).

Teamwork is an important aspect of nursing. Humor helps foster an atmosphere of teamwork.

According to Robinson (1991), one intensive care unit that had no staff turnover in 7 years reported that the climate of humor was one factor in the productivity and effectiveness of the group. Without humor, work would be colorless and devoid of enjoyment.

Kinde (2002) offers a suggestion for helping nurses build humor into the workplace. He suggests taking a comment that someone makes and creating a "shopping list" of events. The example he uses is to take a comment such as "This place is a war zone" and make two separate lists. One list can be called "hospital things" and the other can be called "military things." The next step is to brainstorm by making the lists as long as possible. Everyone can take part in the development of the list.

Kinde (2002) shares his list of "Ten Ways a Hospital is Like the Military." Table 6-1 highlights excerpts from this list.

TABLE 6-1: BUILDING WORKPLACE HUMOR

Excerpts from "Ten Ways a Hospital is Like the Military."

- In the military, soldiers take orders from people with silver and gold on their shoulders. In a hospital, nurses take orders from people with silver and gold in their wallets.

- When discharged from the hospital after a lower GI series, you get the GI bill.

- Nurses, like soldiers, see a lot of privates.

- Nurse training is like boot camp. Never before had you seen so many bald body parts.

- In the military, a fatigue is what you wear. In nursing, it's what wears on you.

(Kinde, 2002. ¶24)

USING HUMOR WITH PATIENTS

Humor helps healthcare providers connect with their patients. You say you are not one to tell jokes because you never remember the punch line?

Have no fear, jokes are not the only way to use humor with patients. Humor can sometimes be found in an off-hand remark that comes out funny. Sometimes it is deliberate. Other times, humor involves recognizing a humor attempt by a patient.

According to Wooten (1996), the Iowa Intervention Project has identified at least 357 nursing intervention classifications (NIC). One of these is humor. The operational definition of humor given to this NIC is, "Facilitating the patient to perceive, appreciate and express what is funny, amusing or ludicrous in order to establish relationships, relieve tension, release anger, facilitate learning or cope with painful feelings" (p. 47).

A study by Adamle (2001) found that humor in hospice settings was more often initiated by the patient than the nurse. Humor gives patients an alternate way of looking at their situation and helps them explore new coping skills and gain some element of control (Bellert, 1989).

A study by Lippert (2001), which investigated the use of humor in a long-term care setting, found that humor was more often initiated by nurses in this setting. The humorous exchanges tended to occur during care tasks or routine rituals, such as medication passes or meals. The most common type of humor used was conversational humor. Even with patients who have dementia, the use of humor, and especially the response of laughter, helps form a connection between patients and nurses.

In a study involving analysis of nurses' diaries, Astedt-Kurkie and Isola (2001) found that humor could be initiated by both the nurse and the patient. Because observation was not a part of this study, it is difficult to know who was more likely to initiate the humor. However, humor seemed to help nurses and patients deal with routine care, unpleasant procedures, embarrassing events, and difficult situations. Humor also functioned as a way for people to admit that they did not know everything without "losing face" (Astedt-Kurkie & Isola, 2001, p. 457).

In reviewing these studies, a question arises: Does the setting influence who initiates the humor? In Adamle's (2001) study, did the nurses hold back and wait to see if the patient would use humor because the nurses were dealing with patients who were dying? Were the nurses demonstrating caution and respect for their patient's needs and emotional status? In Lippert's (2001) study, did the nurses initiate humor because it was a situation in which a rapport had been established and the social norm allowed nurses to feel comfortable with using humor? These questions raise issues for further study and further thought by nurses. When is it appropriate to use humor? How can nurses know when humor will be appropriate and appreciated? Sometimes they do not, and humor might be used inappropriately. In this situation, the nurse must be sensitive enough to recognize it and apologize.

Humor can help establish rapport with a patient, or it can help enhance an established rapport. It is important to note that the nurse needs to be sensitive to a patient's emotional state if she or he is going to be the initiator of humor. Some people prefer to be the initiators of humor, and ill-timed humor can be hurtful.

One thing nurses are commonly cautioned about in nursing school is offering too much self-disclosure. Humor is one method of self-disclosure that can help build a bond in a way that is not threatening to the nurse. For example, a nurse can share with a patient a situation similar to the one the patient is dealing with but with a humorous overtone. This communication can help the patient put his or her situation into perspective without threat. Humor may also work as a teaching tool.

Personal Insight

I am a cancer survivor and a firm believer in the use of humor as a coping mechanism. It is not uncommon that someone will refer a patient with breast cancer to me. One of the things I do is share my own struggle — including the ups and downs of dealing with a potentially life-threatening disease. I also share my strong belief that humor works as an effective coping mechanism, and that I now sport a smiley face on my reconstructed breast. A number of patients have shared how helpful it was to look at the lighter side of breast cancer and how the conversation reminded them to find the humor in their own situation.

Humor can be used to ask questions about sensitive subjects, such as dying, sexuality, loss of control, and suicide. "Humor becomes the 'how' of asking and laughter becomes the language of closeness" (Gullickson, 1995). As noted by Adamle (2001), even during the terminal phase of life, humor serves as a means of allowing the patient, the family, and the nurse to view the patient as still possessing life.

This need to still be viewed as being alive is apparent in the following interchange between a nurse and a hospice patient. The patient was an elderly gentleman who was an avid fisherman. He was admitted to hospice with metastatic colon cancer and was in a lot of pain. On one of the visits, the nurse asked, "How have you been feeling? Anxious at all?" The following discussion ensued (Adamle, 2001, p. 117):

Patient: I am anxious to get the boat out, anxious to have warmer weather, anxious to drop my line in the lake, anxious to catch my first fish this year! Next week you'll have to do your visit down at the lake 'cause I'll be there!

Family: I'll drive her down there to see you. (rolls her eyes and laugh)

Nurse: That's a deal! (laughs)

Dementia is a concern for many people as they age. The following interchange took place between a hospice nurse and a 71-year-old female who was living in a nursing home (Adamle, 2001, p. 117):

Nurse: I have to write this down (vital signs). I'm getting so forgetful. If I don't write it down, I'll loose track of what I'm doing! (laughs and holds her head in her hands)

Patient: Oh please, don't talk to me about that, honey. (laughs) Just you wait until you are my age and in my shape! (laughs)

Humor can also work to decrease a stressful situation, as in the continued exchange with the above patient. When the nurse asked if the patient had any new problems the nurse should know about, the patient recounted a story of being left on the bedpan. She put her light on and no one came, so the patient called the front desk on her personal phone and asked if someone could get her off the pan or if she should call 911 (Adamle, 2001, p. 118).

Personal Insight

I used humor to cope with emotions that defied words following my mastectomy and reconstructive surgery. I explain it this way:

It was the second night after surgery and I needed to go to the bathroom. Being the "good nurse," I got out of bed, unplugged my IV pump, and got into the bathroom. Since I had a tramflap, I was unable to comfortably put my feet on the floor, so I pulled up the shower seat and was sitting there trying to void when the tears started. I cried and cried, and suddenly I thought, if anyone comes in right now and sees me, I will look so ridiculous. At that, I started to laugh at the absurdity of the situation.

The ability to laugh at the situation, to see the funny side of a situation that was difficult, helped me get through that particular event and the night. It helped make the situation seem less distressing. Today, it serves as a piece of information that can be shared.

At a humor conference, a well-known humor presenter was sharing an experience he had when he was asked to talk to a group of patients with cancer. He wanted to make sure that the group leader understood that he was a humorist and that he talked about humor. He wondered if humor would be an appropriate topic for people dealing with cancer. The group leader reassured him that he knew that the presenter talked about humor and that was why he had been asked to present. As the group began, the presenter became concerned. The group members sat in a circle, and each person shared a little about his or her story. As the gravity of the disease processes were shared, the presenter prayed that God would reveal some way of presenting his material without seeming inappropriate. Finally, one man said, "I was diagnosed with cancer and told I had about 6 months to live, so I gave away all my winter clothes, but I have lived long enough to see another winter, and I have nothing warm to wear." At that, everyone began to laugh. Finally, the presenter started his shtick. The group was laughing uproariously when a woman stuck her head in the door. "I'm leading a group for bereaved individuals next door," she began. The presenter thought, "Now I've done it." Then she continued, "We would like to know if we can come join you." They joined the group and afterwards thanked the presenter for a chance to be able to laugh.

Nurses are commonly taught the proper way of administering medications; however, few are taught the proper way to administer humor. Karyn Buxman (1996), a nurse humorist, talks about the five rights of humor administration. They include the Right Patient, the Right Type of humor, the Right Time, the Right Amount, and the Right Route (Table 6-2).

Dan Gascon (1998) lists 12 things that he says "humor gives where illness lives." According to Gascon, humor

1. helps individuals step back from their illnesses.

2. helps patients gain perspective.

3. shows patients that there is more to life than just physical disabilities.

4. opens minds to realities that are fun, joyous, and light.

5. makes people smile.

6. achieves states that are tranquil, flowing, and worry-free.

7. validates that, although a person may be seriously ill or in the process of dying, at the moment, they are alive!

8. involves everyone in conversation.

9. insulates against loneliness and fear.

10. is a sign of approval, caring, compassion, and connection.

TABLE 6-2: THE FIVE RIGHTS OF HUMOR ADMINISTRATION

1.	**Right Patient**	For some patients, humor is inappropriate or unhelpful. Some patients do not appreciate humor.
2.	**Right Type**	At times, certain types of humor, such as gallows or black humor, may be in poor taste. Sarcastic humor aimed at the patient in the form of a put-down is also inappropriate.
3.	**Right Time**	Timing is crucial. Humor might be appropriate with patients who have mild to moderate anxiety but inappropriate during a crisis or when the anxiety level of the patient is high. At times of high anxiety, humor may be distracting and offensive.
4.	**Right Amount**	Too much of a good thing ruins effectiveness. Continued attempts at joking and humor may be overwhelming and annoying.
5.	**Right Route**	Humor does not have to come in the form of jokes. In some cases, being able to laugh at oneself or the situation is most effective. Spontaneous humor is often appreciated more than joke telling.

(Buxman, 1996)

11. loves them with lightness and joy.

12. lifts the spirit and speeds recovery!

(Gascom, 1998, ¶5)

USING HUMOR WITH DYING PATIENTS

As previously noted, humor is appropriate for use with patients who are dying. In most cases, dying people still want to be a part of life for as long as they can. As Alan Klein (1998) stated in his book *The Courage to Laugh,* which shares anecdotal stories about humor in the face of death and dying, "[Humor] is nature's way of giving us a perspective on a situation and allowing us to rise above it. Humor helps us keep our balance when life throws us a curve ball" (p. 4)

There is nothing funny about dying or the grief of impending loss of a loved one. However, funny things happen as a person dies. It is up to those involved in the situation to decide whether they want to see the humor. Remember, however, that what might be humorous to one person may not be to another. Humor can be hurtful or inappropriate. However, as noted earlier, humor can also be helpful and appreciated. For example, one patient responded to humor with the comment, "I'm so tired of everyone being so solemn. It is great to be able to laugh."

Certain barriers make the use of humor during death and dying uncommon. These barriers include

- the American cultural view that death is a negative experience to be feared

- the belief that dying people should be approached with a muted display of positive emotions (Herth, 1995)

- the physical, emotional, and social pain and loss that dying evokes

- the physical deterioration that affects dying people and, in return, affects all those connected with them.

A descriptive study by Herth (1995) involving 14 terminally ill adults indicated that sharing positive feelings helped the participants feel "like a real person again" (p. 220). The positive effects of humor as seen by these participants are as follows:

- It helped maintain a sense of belonging.

- It promoted relaxation.

- It helped alter perceptions.

- It offered a feeling of warmth, a sense of light-heartedness, and delight.

- Occasionally, it offered hearty laughter.

- It was a "life-enricher" and a "life-enhancer."

USING HUMOR WITH FAMILY CAREGIVERS

Humor can help a nurse connect with a patient's significant others. Remember that appropriate humor can be a good means of communication. It can break down barriers and relieve tension. Caregivers may feel powerlessness, fear, frustration, anxiety, or any number of negative emotions when a loved one is ill. The use of humor can assist the caregiver in dealing with all of these emotions. It can sometimes be hard to see the humor in a situation, and the caregiver might need a little assistance. Other times, humor is inappropriate. The nurse needs to be sensitive to the appropriateness and timing of humor.

When a situation seems to be grave, the use of humor may be inappropriate. However, humor may also be a way of lightening up a situation. For example, when my husband was dying, humor was an appropriate tool to lessen the anticipatory grief. However, ill-timed humor might have been hurtful. Being alert to both patient and caregiver needs allows a nurse to help the patient and the family during a difficult time. An example of this occurred with the 70-year-old avid fisherman mentioned earlier. During a revisit, the nurse asked about anxiety:

Nurse: How have you been feeling? Anxious at all?

Wife: Which one of us? (laughs)

This exchange could be a good opportunity for the nurse to explore the family members' level of anxiety. Awareness of the underlying messages behind the humor can allow the nurse to design interventions useful to the patient and family.

Family members may use humor as a means of helping the healthcare provider as well. After my husband died, the doctor who admitted him came onto the unit. I could see that the doctor was shaken by the death, and he confirmed this when he said, "This should never have happened. We should have been able to turn around his idiopathic thrombocytopenia." Feeling that I needed to do something for both the doctor and myself, I said: "If he had lived, he would have had one problem after another; then he would have gotten depressed, and then I would have had to kill him. So he saved me from going to jail." At that, the doctor and I chuckled, and the tension of us two grievers decreased.

HUMOR ASSESSMENT

Nurses are always doing assessments of different body systems and mental capacities. What about doing a humor assessment? The humor assessment helps to discover the type of humor patients use or appreciate as a means of designing humor interventions appropriate for the patient. Table 6-3 includes some questions that can be asked. These are only suggested questions. It is up to each nurse to decide which questions and how many are appropriate for a particular patient.

Part of a humor assessment involves being cognitively aware of the patient's response to humor. Does the patient smile or laugh at lighthearted remarks? Does the patient watch sitcoms on television? Does the patient seem to use humor as an avoidance or defense mechanism? Because humor can be used inappropriately to avoid problem solv-

TABLE 6-3: HUMOR ASSESSMENT QUESTIONS
• What importance does humor play in your life?
• What makes you laugh?
• Who makes you laugh?
• Since your illness, do you find yourself using humor more, less, or about the same?
• What is one area of your life to which you would like to add humor?
• Do you consider humor a source of relaxation?
• What kind of jokes do you like?
• What does the phrase "laughter is the best medicine" mean to you?
• What type of humor offends you?
• What is your favorite sitcom? What is it about that show that makes you laugh?

ing or dealing with feelings, the nurse must assess the possibility that the patient is using defensive humor, which might interfere with coping.

THE NEGATIVE SIDE OF HUMOR

As previously mentioned, humor can have negative effects. This section explores some of the inappropriate uses of humor. Harvey (1998) discusses a 1956 study by Levine, who found that there are three possible responses to humor:

1. It evokes no anxiety and, therefore, the listener responds with indifference.

2. It evokes and then immediately dissipates anxiety. The listener considers the humor amusing or funny.

3. It arouses anxiety without decreasing it. The listener does not find the humor funny and may even feel disgust or embarrassment.

One type of humor that can be destructive is hostile humor. Examples of hostile humor include cultural slurs, or comments about a person's behavior.

Hostile humor may also be used to help express anger, such as the patient who wanted to know if she should call 911 in order to be removed from the bedpan. However, if the patient's nurse was tired and frustrated, she may not have seen the humor in this comment. Here is another example: An alert patient broke her leg while on vacation. She was admitted to a nursing home for rehabilitation but was unable to get out of bed without assistance. Her roommate, a resident with dementia, was trying to get out of bed to go to the bathroom. The patient put on her light but no one came. She called for help and still no one came. Fearful that her roommate would fall and injure herself, the patient started throwing things against the wall to make noise until the aide came in. Instead of seeing the humor in the situation, the aide told the woman that her behavior was inappropriate. In telling the story to the nurse the next day, the resident and the nurse had a good laugh.

Some gallows humor can be hurtful or offensive to others. The term "GOMER" is one example of this type of gallows humor. Short for "Get Out of My Emergency Room," GOMER was coined by Dr. Samuel Shem, who wrote a "hilarious and often heart-rending book called House of God" (Wooten, 1996, pg. 25). The term was originally used to refer to patients who were very ill, uncooperative, unappreciative of help, or confused but is now commonly used to describe patients who are in a vegetative state. Although gallows humor can help care providers deal with difficult events and situations, it can have a negative effect on the people to whom it is directed and can lead to insult and alienation (Harvey, 1998).

Humor is sometimes used to avoid the therapeutic process or avoid painful issues. This may take the form of "scapegoating," or aiming the humor at one person in the group. This can be hurtful and nonproductive. Humor is also inappropriate if the receiver of the message does not know if the speaker is serious or joking.

If a nurse has doubts about how another person might receive a joke, it is best not to tell it. Before saying something that might be hurtful, the nurse should think about how he or she might feel in a similar situation. It is one thing for an individual who has a disability to make a joke about the disability. This type of self-defacing humor might help relieve tension. However, if an able-bodied person makes the same joke, the comment might be considered a slur.

STORIES FROM THE FIELD

The following examples illustrate how humor has been used to help people deal with illness or hospitalization.

Bob, a man in his 50s, had a tumor on his knee that required surgery. Being aware of the power of laughter in the healing process, the patient asked Annette Goodheart, a laughter therapist, to visit him right after surgery. He had a large 10-in. to 12-in. suture around his knee, but his knee was wrapped in such a manner that he was able to remove a portion of the outer bandage. Dr. Goodheart had him gently press around the incision area and say, "Ow!" A pillow was ready so that if a big "Ow!" came out, the patient could stifle the sound and not alarm the hospital staff.

As he pressed around the incision and said "Ow," he laughed. The more he pressed and the more he said "Ow," the more he laughed. In between the laughter, he related the events of the surgery. By processing the emotions that occurred during surgery, he prevented tension from storing around the traumatized area, allowing his body's healing mechanisms to function faster and more freely.

After about half an hour, the patient was able to endure more and more pressure without feeling pain. At this point, the surgeon came in to see how the patient was doing. He came toward the bed and said, "Bob, how are you feeling?" Bob kicked out his leg. The surgeon was so shocked, he almost fell over backward. Bob was on his feet within several hours, walking around the hall. He reported that the surgeon was astounded by the rate of his recovery. (Goodheart, 1994, p. 59-60)

The following story came from personal communication with an acquaintance.

Personally, I am not naturally inclined to see humor in things and tend to be too serious. It always takes me longer to get a joke. Recently, my cage has been rattled to give me a wake-up call. Surgery for a skin graft in January left me with unhappy results of the loss of 60% of the graft. After trying everything medically possible, along with prayer, a friend suggested I try humor. I now intentionally factor in times of watching comedy and laughing every day. The graft is healing, and a really neat benefit of more wholesome relationships with my family has resulted.

The following story was received via e-mail.

An old man often sat at a specific corner table with his friends. He rarely went more than 10 or 15 minutes without laughing. When asked how he managed to stay in such a wonderful mood all the time, he responded that his laughter did not always mean he was in a good mood. He explained that he laughed for two reasons. One was to get into a good mood. He lived alone and did not like it. He knew that laughter would lift his spirits, so he forced himself to laugh until he really was feeling good. The other reason was that he had arthritis and had a lot of aches and pains. One day he and his friends were doubling up with laughter about pranks they had played when they were kids. He discovered that his arthritis pain

had disappeared during the laughter and did not show up again until an hour later. From that day on, he was a laugher. It was his way of managing pain and taking control in a way that improved his quality of life.

Being able to find humor in different situations is important. The following are stories that nurses have shared about funny things that have happened at work.

I was admitting a patient one night and asking the usual questions on the admit form. When I asked my patient if she had any allergies, she informed me that she was allergic to Ipecac. Seems it made her throw up every time she took it.

H. Sox

When I worked in traumatic brain injury rehabilitation, a nurse briefly placed a bisacodyl suppository at a patient's bedside. He promptly ate it.

We called the local poison control center hotline to find out what to do. After listening to our story, the nurse at the hotline reassured us. She said, "This, too, will pass."

K. Dunn

One day in the OR, I was holding a patient in a sitting position while the anesthesiologist was administering a spinal anesthetic for a TURP. Warning the patient of the impending injection, the physician said, "Little prick here!"

The patient, who was bending over, staring at his crotch, said, "Yeah, I know. It's been that way all my life."

M. Wren

SUMMARY

Humor is an important part of healthcare. The anecdotal stories in this chapter present a personal picture from nurses' and patients' views of the effectiveness of humor in the healthcare setting.

These stories present a colorful picture of how humor can be effective for the patient and the nurse. Studies show that humor helps patients deal with the difficulties of illness and helps form a connection between nurse and patient. Some studies have explored who commonly initiates humor in the healthcare setting—sometimes it is the nurse and sometimes it is the patient. Deciding when it is appropriate to use humor can be challenging. Rapport and sensitivity are keys in deciding if humor is appropriate. Humor initiated by the patient is commonly a clue that humor is an acceptable response. However, it is important to remember that, although humor can be healing and form a connection between people, it can also be hurtful. Being sensitive, alert to when humor might be helpful, and spontaneous is important.

CHAPTER 6
Questions 46-54

46. According to Buxman, the three main functions of humor in healthcare are

   a. psychological, social, spiritual.

   b. spiritual, social, communication.

   c. psychological, social, communication.

   d. focal, psychological, social.

47. One appropriate way to diffuse tension at work is to

   a. scream.

   b. share a joke.

   c. mumble to yourself.

   d. throw something.

48. When a person shares humor with someone they are angry at

   a. it momentarily defuses the situation.

   b. the other person feels put down.

   c. the superiority theory is activated.

   d. distancing can occur.

49. A common form of humor between nurses in high-stress areas is

   a. incongruent-resolution humor.

   b. illusion formation.

   c. gallows humor.

   d. comical wordplay.

50. A patient who recently sustained an injury that left her paraplegic states with a laugh, "I guess I won't be needing those high heels I just bought." The nurse's best response would be to

   a. laugh at her.

   b. ask what she would like to do with them.

   c. say, "It sounds like you are concerned about the changes in your life."

   d. walk out of the room without saying or doing anything.

51. Humor has been identified and given an operational definition by the

   a. Nursing Intervention Classifications.

   b. Nursing Outcome Classifications.

   c. North American Nursing Diagnosis Association.

   d. American Holistic Nurses Association.

52. The study by Adamle that looked at humor in the hospice setting discovered that humor was initiated most often by

   a. the nurse.

   b. the patient.

   c. the family.

   d. the nurse's aide.

53. The purpose of a humor assessment is to

   a. discover what jokes the patient already knows.

   b. get the patient thinking about using humor to cope.

   c. prove that patients use humor.

   d. discover the type of humor that might be appropriate for the patient.

Situation

A nurse is admitting a Jewish woman to the hospital. The woman is wearing designer clothes. To establish rapport, the nurse tells an ethnic joke about a Jewish princess. Instead of laughing, the patient looks offended. Later, the nurse overhears the patient tell the same joke to a Jewish friend, who laughs at the joke.

Based on this situation, respond to question 54 below.

54. The difference between the patient's two responses is best explained by

   a. the patient thinking she missed something because she did not see anything funny in the joke, so she decided to see how her friend reacted.

   b. the patient did not understand the joke and hoped her friend could explain it to her.

   c. the patient being too nervous to appreciate the humor at the time of admission.

   d. the tendency for self-defacing humor to be better accepted by the receiver when it is shared with others of the same ethnic or situational group.

CHAPTER 7

THE USE OF HUMOR IN CRISES AND DISASTER SITUATIONS

If you can find humor in it, you can survive it.

Bill Cosby

CHAPTER OBJECTIVE

After completing this chapter, the reader will be able to discuss the role of humor in crises and disaster situations and discern when healthcare provider intervention is most appropriate.

LEARNING OBJECTIVES

After studying this chapter, the reader will be able to

1. identify the psychological factors that affect humor reactions during crises.

2. list ways individuals have found to incorporate humor into their lives following a crisis.

3. explain the healthcare provider's role in crisis humor.

4. describe how humor helped prisoners of war (POWs) and other victims of war survive imprisonment and torture.

INTRODUCTION

Some people feel that humor is inappropriate during a crisis; however, others find that humor helps them put perspective on the crisis (Buxman, 2001; Frankl, 1963; Henman, 2001; Ritz, 1995; Sutlanoff, 1995; Wooten & Dunkelblau, 2001). Ritz (1995) notes that a disaster occurs in the world every 8½ days. With the ongoing crisis in the Middle East, disasters seem to occur on an almost daily basis nowadays. It can be difficult for people to see any humor in a crisis. One crisis that almost every person in the United States can identify with occurred September 11, 2001. This chapter looks at how individuals resolved their experiences of September 11, as well as other crises such as the Holocaust, natural disasters, and being POWs.

SEPTEMBER 11

The tragedy that occurred on September 11, 2001, was so horrendous that it took a while before humor returned, even for those people who use humor as a coping mechanism. Klein (2001) notes that one news reporter stated it took 5 days, 2 hours, 8 minutes, and 1 second from the time the first plane hit the World Trade Center for the first attempts at humor to appear on the Internet. Buxman (2001), a registered nurse who presents humor and stress management workshops, notes that people mentioned they wanted to laugh but could not or were afraid to because of what others would think. Wooten and Dunkelblau (2001) note, "On September 11, Americans lost their will to laugh."

Sultanoff (1995) states that "during a crisis humor is often experienced and perceived by individuals immersed in the crisis as insensitive and even hurtful." He theorizes that individuals closest to the crisis are "more likely to integrate the crisis into their internal emotional being" (¶2). Wooten and Dunkelblau (2001) explain that there is an inability to separate the inner emotional self from the emotional pain of the event. As distance from the crisis occurs, individuals are less likely to experience the merging of self with the crisis and are more able to experience humor aimed at the crisis.

The following story exemplifies how those involved in a crisis might be able to use humor.

A group of office workers at the World Trade Center were running down flight after flight of stairs, not knowing if they had the strength to continue. They reached the 11th floor feeling exhausted and as if they could not go on. Then one woman suggested they pretend it was New Year's Eve and start the countdown. En masse, they began a countdown with each flight of stairs and shouted out "10, 9, 8, 7, 6, 5, 4, 3, 2, 1." Encouraged by the levity, they all made it to the street and safety.

It was so difficult to find things to laugh at during the first few days following the attack on the World Trade Center that even Jay Leno had difficulty finding material to use. Comics were careful and cautious about what they said. News items that had appeared before September 11 became material for gags. Comics used opening lines such as, "Remember the good ole days of the West Nile virus?" Jay Leno got laughs with "America must now protect itself from angry religious extremists. But enough about Jerry Falwell."

DISASTER SITUATIONS

Sandra Ritz (1995) is a nurse who has studied survivor humor following disasters. As Ritz (1995) mentions, nurses are commonly involved in disasters, either as disaster workers or as survivors of the disaster. Disasters include hurricanes, earthquakes, tornados, volcanic eruptions, floods, war, terrorist attacks, riots, radiation accidents, airplane crashes, multivehicle accidents, epidemics, or any number of unexpected natural or man-made catastrophes. When a nurse deals with a disaster, flexibility and creativity are essential skills . The nurse has little time to worry about what might be happening outside the immediate situation. What must have occurred for the nurses involved in September 11, especially those who lived near the World Trade Center?

Humor After a Disaster

As Ritz (1995) notes, the use of humor in a disaster situation can work as a coping strategy by relieving tension, managing stress, and reframing perspective. Sultanoff (1995) notes that humor provides a perspective and helps us deal with emotional turmoil.

As Jay Leno said following a California earthquake:

It's not all tragedy. You have to like the way the earthquake has brought this city together. I was driving down Sunset Boulevard and I noticed a white man, a black man, and a Hispanic man all looting together. (Ritz, 1995, p. 198)

Gallows humor is the most common form of humor used in disaster situations. Ritz (1995) refers to gallows humor as "survivor humor." She states that "survivor humor is an active defense mechanism that helps to cope with threats and fears instead of surrendering to them" (p. 200). It may be difficult for those not directly affected by the disaster to understand the humor, but for the person affected, humor can be used to shock oneself out of horror and anxiety.

One example of survivor humor occurred during Santa Barbara fires in 1994. In the neighborhoods where all of the homes were burned except for the fireplaces, people wore t-shirts that read: "My chimney is bigger than your chimney!" (Ritz, 1995, p. 200).

The Disaster Relief Act of 1974 recognized the mental health needs of those involved in disasters.

"This act mandates that the National Institute of Mental Health provide mental health crisis counseling services and training as part of the disaster relief effort" (Ritz, 1995, p. 204). The biggest problems following a disaster are problems of living and readjustment. However, people are relatively resilient, and most people recover from the temporary emotional stress of a crisis. Grief reactions are also a common and normal part of a crisis or disaster. After all, a peson experiences loss when his or her home is damaged or destroyed by fire, earthquake, or another natural disaster.

According to Ritz (1995), three factors are essential in survivor recovery: (1) relief from stress; (2) talking about the experience; (3) passage of time.

We know humor is effective for stress relief; yet, until Ritz's (1995) study, there was very little research on the use of humor in disaster situations. The emphasis in the literature has been placed on the human service workers supporting usual coping mechanisms rather than looking at how humor might be utilized (Farberow & Fredrick, 1978, cited in Ritz, 1995). Humor assists in adaptation to change following a crisis and is an important element in long-term recovery for disaster survivors.

Ritz (1995) discusses the four emotional phases survivors experience after a disaster: heroic, honeymoon, disillusionment, and reconstruction. During the heroic phase, survival is the basic concern. The honeymoon phase occurs 1 week to 3 to 6 months after the disaster and involves recovery of optimism. The disillusionment phase occurs 2 months to 2 years after the disaster. During this phase, anger, resentment, and disappointment are common. The person may feel oppressed by the agencies and organizations that have invaded the community. The reconstruction phase is a period of recovery, rebuilding, and acceptance.

It was mentioned previously that passage of time helps heal those affected by a disaster. Leigh (2001) notes that humor tends to return as time passes and the distance from the crisis grows longer.

Different types of humor are prevalent during each of the emotional phases experienced after a disaster. Table 7-1 indicates the types of humor that are commonly used during those phases.

TABLE 7-1: DISASTER PHASES AND HUMOR USAGE	
PHASE	**TYPE OF HUMOR USED**
Heroic	Spontaneous
Honeymoon	Hopeful, reflects a sense of optimism
Disillusionment	Negative humor aimed at outside assistance, sarcastic humor
Reconstruction	Reflects a sense of community
(Ritz, 1995)	

During the *heroic phase*, humor is spontaneously produced by the survivor to relieve tension and overcome fear (Ritz, 1995). One example was shared by Ritz (cited in Klein, 1998): "Two hikers, caught on the coast trail of Kauai when Hurricane Iniki struck, sang the theme song from 'Gilligan's Island.' They kept up their spirits and dispelled their anxiety by reframing the situation in a comical format" (p. 161).

Most of the disaster-type humor occurs during the *honeymoon phase*. The humor during this phase is typically positive and hopeful. It reflects a sense of optimism. An example of this type of humor in the previous example was a t-shirt that read, "Landscaped by Iniki" (Klein, 1998).

During the *disillusionment phase*, the type of humor that might now be appropriate in earlier phases might now be misinterpreted because the survivors are feeling bitter. During the reconstruction phase, humor returns slowly. The humor might portray the disillusionment felt with the disaster assistance provided. For example, after Hurricane Andrew hit the Florida coast, some people wore t-shirts that read, "I survived Hurricane Andrew, but FEMA [the Federal Emergency Management Agency] is killing me" (Klein, 1998, p. 161).

Another example of disillusionment humor occurred following Hurricane Iniki in 1992 in Kauai. This example demonstrates how language and cultural differences between survivors and relief workers can increase frustration and perhaps cause anger. A comedy skit on KONG radio went as follows:

Cheryl: Hi, I'm Cheryl from Cold-Hand Insurance Company. I'm here to look at your home. Are you Mrs. Kam-a-ka?"

Mrs. Kamaka: No, that's Mrs. Kamaka . . . Never mind girl, you call me Auntie . . .

Cheryl: Tell me, was there any damage done to your davenport, your living area, your veranda, your portecochère, or your daybed?

Mrs. Kamaka: No, but I had damage on top of my sofa, inside da parlor, da lanai, da garage, and on top of my pune'e. (Pune'e is Hawaiian for couch or single bed.) (cited in Ritz, 1995, p. 201)

Reconstruction humor commonly reflects a sense of community as people begin to rebuild their lives. An example of this type of humor occurred after the multiple disasters that affected the southern California area. Residents were heard to remark, "Los Angeles has four distinct seasons: Earthquake, Flood, Firestorm, and Mud Slide" (Klein, 1998).

Karyn Buxman (2001) notes

Nineteen ninety-three marked "the Flood of 500 Years" on the Mississippi River. Communities along the entire river experienced flooding, destruction of property, loss of homes and jobs, and sometimes death. Yet, humor marked the will of people to keep their spirits afloat, not to be oppressed and depressed by the Muddy Mississippi. In Iowa, the Des Moines Register held a contest, "I'm a Floody Mess," where contestants tried to one-up one another with descriptions of their misery. When the local water system failed as a result of the flood, and running water for drinking and bathing was no longer an option, one contestant wrote, "I smell so bad that my Sure deodorant is undecided." (¶ 13)

After the 1993 Midwest flood, the following billboards were spotted (cited in Klein, 1998):

Questions about the weather?
Call 1-800-NOAH

Welcome to Missouri,
The Row Me State
(Missouri is known as "The Show-Me State")

The weather lately gives a whole new meaning
to Roe vs. Wade

The above examples also point out the use of community resources, (in this case, the media), in helping support other members of the community. In a general disaster, having others in the situation who can understand the frustrations of the loss as well as the frustrations of dealing with disaster relief organizations helps survivors through the experience.

DISASTER WORKERS' RESPONSE

Research shows that many disaster and emergency workers have at least one symptom of post-traumatic stress disorder (PTSD). To address disaster stress, Critical Incident Stress Debriefing (CISD) was developed. The purpose of CISD is to lessen the impact of an event to which workers have been called out to assist. Training programs and simulation exercises aim at preventing disaster workers from experiencing stress in the first place. Ritz (1995) notes that the use of humor for stress reduction is not addressed in most stress-management courses' lists of stress-reduction techniques. Humor is rarely mentioned in federal or state disaster training booklets. Although one might find mention of "laughter is the best medicine" or "avoid grim humor."

Just as disaster survivors attempt to adapt and manage, so do disaster relief workers and nurses. Nurses may be directly affected by being survivors, or indirectly affected by needing to care for survivors. Disaster relief workers and nurses giving care need effective methods of coping, just as those directly affected by the disaster do. Nurses and disaster relief workers can use humor to decrease their own stress and connect with other members of the disaster relief team. As McGhee (n.d.) has been told by people at FEMA conferences, state emergency response teams, and police, "If we didn't laugh at some of the things that happen, we'd never survive this job." Nurses who work in emergency rooms, critical care units, and other units where life and death often hang in the balance have shared that they use black humor to survive.

Some of the jokes that people make after disasters may be interpreted as sick and inappropriate by others. For example, after an emergency response team spent the morning putting bodies from a plane crash in bags, someone said, "The bag lunches are here."

After the Delta crash in the 1980s, the following comments were heard for a number of years among relief workers:

> At Delta, we now offer three classes of service: smoking, nonsmoking, and burned beyond recognition.

> Delta now offers you free drinks if you present your dental records when purchasing your ticket.

Nurses who work in disaster situations need to remember that humor can be helpful or hurtful. To use humor effectively, the nurse must assess the survivor's current phase of recovery. The nurse should also keep in mind that the humor appreciated by one person may be different from the humor appreciated by another, depending on what phase of adjustment the two individuals have reached. Inappropriate humor can be more hurtful than helpful. Assessing a patient's needs and survival phase is important in order to design appropriate humor. Being aware of which type of humor is appropriate for which phase of recovery is also important. Humor used therapeutically and judiciously can be helpful for the survivor. Learning to laugh again may be essential for emotional coping.

HUMOR WITH LOSS OF FREEDOM

Captain Gerald Coffee, a former Vietnam POW shared in his book *Beyond Survival*, "Laughter sets the spirit free to move through even the most tragic circumstances. It helps us shake our heads clear, get our feet back under us and restore our sense of balance and purpose. Humor is integral to our peace of mind and ability to go beyond survival" (Coffee, 1990, p. 131).

In Coffee's place of captivity, an old cell had been converted into a shower. On the wall of the shower, the following message appeared: "Smile, you're on Candid Camera." Coffee (1990) states that when he saw this message, "I laughed out loud, enjoying not only the pure humor and incongruity of the situation, but also appreciating the beautiful guy who had mustered the moxie to rise above his own dejection and frustration and pain and guilt to inscribe a line of encouragement to those who would come after him . . . he deserved a medal for it." (p. 131-132).

It is hard to imagine using humor to survive the Holocaust or to survive the tortures of being a POW during the Vietnam War. However, humor is one of the mechanisms people used to survive the horrors of the camps and prisons (Frankl, 1963; Henman, 2001). Humor has given people who were prisoners during war a sense of hope. It also established a bond among the prisoners (Frankl, 1963; Henman, 2001; Klein, 1998).

In his famous book, *Man's Search for Meaning*, Frankl (1963) discusses how even the smallest joke gave Holocaust prisoners such as himself a sense of hope. Humor helped give them something to look forward to each day. Frankl and a fellow prisoner would make up at least one amusing story each day. They joked with one another about life after liberation. One of the stories from the camps is told by a person who was a child at the time of imprisonment. The individual recalls:

> We mimicked top overseers, and I did impersonations about camp life and somebody did a little tap dance — different funny, crazy things. The overseers slipped into the barracks while we weren't looking, and instead of giving us a punishment they were laughing their heads off. I couldn't believe it. One day they were hitting us black and blue, and then they were laughing while we made fun of them. But, you see, in spite of all our agony and pain we never lost our ability to laugh at ourselves and our miserable situation. We had to make jokes to survive and save ourselves from deep depression. (Klein, 1998, p. 149)

Henman (2001) views humor as a determinant of resilience and a method of recovery from the trauma of being a Vietnam POW. Henman did in-depth qualitative interviews with 12 Vietnam POWs who were imprisoned in the "Hanoi Hilton," one of the more notorious prisons. For these men, humor provided a means for building relationships. Humor also became a weapon for fighting back, a means of survival, and a way to remain resilient in the face of severe adversity.

Henman (2001) tells of one POW who realized the value of humor about 10 months after he was captured. The discovery of humor was a turning point for him. The event occurred while he was in solitary confinement. He was peeking through a hole in the wall and watching the guards. One of the guards must have asked for the time, but all he knew was that one guard had asked another guard a question. The POW saw the one guard hand his rifle to the other, then take off his bullet belt and his huge coat, and then reach into his pocket. After struggling with something in his pocket, he pulled out a Baby Ben clock. This struck the prisoner so funny, he started to laugh. He shared:

> He didn't have a watch; he had a Baby Ben clock stuck in his pants pocket. And I'd been beaten pretty severely every day for most of a month, and I was just absolutely rolling on the floor. When this was over, I realized, "I thought I was going to die today; and all I did today was have a good laugh." And so it became apparent to [me] that humor was going to play a major role. (Henman, 2001, p. 86)

Several of the men in Henman's (2001) study told her that they felt humor was so important they would risk torture to tell a joke through the walls to a prisoner whom they felt needed cheering up.

Jeering and finding humor also seemed to be a covert way of fighting back or taking control in a situation in which there seemed to be no personal control. The prisoners established a process by which they could communicate with one another, even when it was dangerous to do so. In an interview for *USA Today* Representative Sam Johnson (R-Texas) talked about a "tap code" that was developed among the prisoners (Kiely, 2003). It was a simplified Morse code that was sometimes whispered from cell to cell, sometimes written in moistened cigarette ash with a bamboo twig on a piece of toilet paper, or even tapped on the wall. Some prisoners were able to tap out 30 words a minute. They also used a broom to sweep messages when they were forced to clean the prison yard. Using this form of communication, the prisoners could chat, share stories, and crack jokes. Retired General Robinson Risner remarked, "Humor was absolutely a necessity" (Kiely, 2003, ¶21).

If humor can promote survival among people undergoing this type of duress, it should be effective for any kind of stressful life event. Nurses are often involved in one way or another with crisis situations. Understanding how humor can be beneficial during those times and how it can be incorporated and encouraged is important. It is also important to think about the following statement made by Captain Coffee to Paul McGhee (2001): "Having some humor skills before being confronted by the adversity played a very important role." With that in mind, incorporating interventions to educate patients about humor might be a way of preventing PTSD when they are confronted with disasters and crises in their lives.

SUMMARY

Even in disaster situations and crises, humor is an important coping mechanism. It has helped people survive terrorist attacks, natural disasters, and war imprisonment. Three factors needed for survivor recovery are relief from stress, talking about the experience, and passage of time. It is known that humor helps to relieve stress. Humor can also help set the stage for survivors to talk about their experiences.

Humor responses vary depending on the phase of disaster recovery the survivor is experiencing. Four phases of emotional recovery have been delineated: heroic, honeymoon, disillusionment, and reconstruction. Each of these phases supports different types of humor. While the disaster survivor is attempting to make sense of the experience, the disaster relief workers are also experiencing a sense of stress as they offer help and relief. The disaster worker and the survivor will see the same situation differently, so humor needs to be used judiciously. Also, the disaster relief worker may need to find an effective way to use humor away from those who are survivors.

Humor has also been demonstrated to be a necessary part of emotional survival for POWs, as demonstrated by POWs of the Vietnam War. Frankl, a survivor of the Holocaust and a psychologist, has written about his experience with humor as a means of giving prisoners a sense of hope.

EXAM QUESTIONS

CHAPTER 7
Questions 55-63

55. During a disaster those directly affected were laughing at a shared experience. The disaster relief worker heard the conversation and thought, "There is nothing funny in what was said." What do you attribute the reason for the relief worker not understanding the humor?

   a. The relief worker has no sense of humor and needs to lighten up.

   b. Those affected by the disaster wanted to shock the relief worker by using humor.

   c. The diaster victims were using humor to deal with their feelings of horror and anxiety.

   d. The disaster victims were not concerned about the effects of the disaster on their lives.

56. Immediately after a tragedy, such as the bombing of the World Trade Center, people respond with

   a. laughter to decrease tension.

   b. wonderment and humor.

   c. shock and the inability to find humor.

   d. sarcastic humor aimed at the perpetrators.

57. The Disaster Relief Act of 1974 provided for

   a. laughter specialists at disaster sites.

   b. humor as a stress reducer.

   c. financial relief for victims.

   d. mental health crisis counseling.

58. The emotional recovery phase that involves optimism is the

   a. heroic phase.

   b. honeymoon phase.

   c. disillusionment phase.

   d. reconstruction phase.

59. The type of disaster humor that reflects a 'sense of community' is in the

   a. heroic phase.

   b. honeymoon phase.

   c. disillusionment phase.

   d. reconstruction phase.

60. Before using humor as a tool to assist patients after a disaster, the first thing a nurse should do is

   a. perform a humor assessment.

   b. assess the patient's phase of recovery.

   c. allow the patient to use humor first.

   d. make sure the patient has received some therapy.

61. Frankl stated that humor gave the prisoners of the Holocaust a sense of

   a. hope.

   b. pride.

   c. compassion.

   d. structure.

62. The most common form of humor seen in disaster situations is

    a. incongruent-resolution humor.
    b. distancing humor.
    c. gallows humor.
    d. cartoons.

63. In disaster situations, it is essential for nurses and disaster workers to

    a. use black humor to cope.
    b. never use laughter with survivors.
    c. find effective ways of coping.
    d. avoid using humor in disasters.

CHAPTER 8

HUMOR IN PSYCHIATRIC SETTINGS

CHAPTER OBJECTIVES

After completing this chapter, the reader will be able to discuss the effective use of humor in psychiatric settings.

LEARNING OBJECTIVES

After studying this chapter, the reader will be able to

1. identify the controversy that exists concerning the use of humor in psychiatric settings.

2. explain ways that humor can be used to diagnose a patient's psychological state.

3. discuss treatment options that include the use of humor in psychiatric settings.

4. recognize behaviors that indicate inappropriate responses to humor.

5. recount appropriate and inappropriate uses of humor in psychiatric settings.

6. discuss the use of humor by caregivers and the impact it has on patient care.

INTRODUCTION

The use of humor in psychiatric settings is a controversial issue. Although humor may be inappropriate with some psychiatric patients, with others, it might be effective, appropriate, and helpful toward recovery. This chapter explores the use of humor in psychiatric settings. Topics include the reason for the controversy over the use of humor, ways to use humor for diagnosis and treatment, and psychiatric patient responses to humor. Appropriate and inappropriate responses and appropriate and inappropriate types of humor are discussed.

THE CONTROVERSY

The use of humor in therapy originally came from classical psychoanalysts (Robinson, 1991), who commonly follow the teachings of Freud. Interestingly, Freud was a pioneer in the area of humor and psychology. However, as Robinson (1991) notes, Freud's concentration on hostile wit rather than positive aspects of humor might be the cause of the modern controversy.

Mark Darby (1996), a psychiatric nurse, shares a story concerning the response of one of his co-workers when she witnessed his use of humor with a patient. The coworker pulled him aside and berated him for telling the patient a joke. She wanted to know, "How can we get patients to trust us if we laugh at them?" (p. 20). She continued to lecture him about appropriate etiquette with patients, which did not include room for even a good chuckle. The coworker was right in that trust is essential; however she was wrong in thinking that laughter and humor would destroy trust and rapport. There is a big difference between laughing with someone and laughing at someone. Humor used to laugh with someone establishes a connection between the parties involved.

Some mental health care providers think that humor can be destructive to the therapeutic environment. This can be true if humor is used inappropriately. Others think that humor can be used to mask hostility and can be harmful if used incorrectly. Of course, inappropriate humor can be destructive to any therapeutic environment, not just the mental health environment. In contrast, humor used appropriately eases tension and can express warmth and caring.

One study cited in Robinson (1991) found that patients with reactive depression (those who experience depression in response to a situation) responded to humor better than patients with psychotic depression. Patients with schizophrenic reactions showed increased ideation. Robinson (1991) mentions, "Although humor may facilitate the flow of free associations, it may block or arrest the patient's spontaneous stream of thought and may also confuse the patient as to whether the therapist is serious or 'only joking'" (p. 102).

Controversy exists concerning the use of humor with patients who have schizophrenia, especially paranoid schizophrenics who might think the nurse or care provider is laughing at them. In a qualitative study by Struthers (1999) on the use of humor by community psychiatric nurses, few of the nurses interviewed said they would not use humor with patients who demonstrated suspicious or paranoid behavior. A study by Gelkopf, Sigal, and Kramer (1994) found that positive humor creates a positive atmosphere between patients and staff.

Interestingly, although controversy surrounds the use of humor in therapy, in a study by Haig (1988), almost 90% of therapists questioned said humor arose sometime during therapy, and 81% said they introduced jokes or humorous remarks during the therapy sessions. They reported they were most likely to use humor with patients who were anxious. The therapists also reported using humor with patients with obsessive disorders, personality disorders, and depression. They would occasionally introduce humor with psychotic patients.

As research continues on the use of humor in mental healthcare, it is hoped that the controversy concerning its use will decrease. A better question than should humor be used in mental health settings is how can humor be used effectively and with which type of patients is it most effective?

HUMOR AS A DIAGNOSTIC TOOL

Although humor is not an effective measure of a psychological illness, it can be used as a means of assessing a patient's psychological state (Sultanoff, 2000).

Provine (2000a) discusses the inappropriate laughter that occurs in some subtypes of schizophrenia. The *Diagnostic and Statistical Manual of Mental Disorders* (*DSM-IV*) lists silliness and laughter that are not related to content of speech as one of the symptoms for schizophrenia of the disorganized type. The behavior of inappropriate laughter could help lead to a specific diagnosis of this disorder (Provine, 2000a).

Haig (1988) discusses humor that might indicate an underlying issue that needs to be explored. He shares the story of a young woman whose sense of inferiority became apparent when she mentioned that she had not been born with a "bicycle pump." According to the story, a magician was away from home when his wife was due to give birth. He did not want to inform the audience or let the other performers know so, when the baby was born, he received a note saying, "The bicycle arrived safely, together with a bicycle pump." The young woman's father had wanted a son and she felt that she had not lived up to his expectations because she, unlike the magician's son, was born without a "bicycle pump" (p. 164). The inferiority she felt because she was not born a boy interfered with her attempts to relate to men. The sharing of this story led to her inferiority issue becoming the focal point of treatment.

According to Haig (1998)

> Spontaneously arising humor and reactions to humor may indicate abnormalities in the underlying mood of the patient. The depressed individual may rarely find anything humorous . . . if he does, the humor is often "black" or tainted with irony... Laughter in the opening session often indicates discomfort or anxiety. Humor that arises suddenly with little apparent relevance to the topic being discussed may indicate denial, with repressed anxiety. (p. 164)

Humor can be a measuring stick for assessing progression in therapy. While working with women who were diagnosed with posttraumatic stress disorder (PTSD), I found that humor was a measuring stick by which my two coleaders could monitor the group's progress. Humor was a tool that was often employed, and those women who were very depressed were less likely to laugh at humorous comments in the beginning of the session. Often, depression had lifted by the end of the session and smiles could be seen.

Sultanoff (2000) shares a story of a woman who felt that bad things happened to her because she was "stupid." He was able to assess her progress in therapy through a humorous statement concerning her sense of being stupid. When she responded to his comment with laughter, he assessed that she had made progress in therapy. If she had not responded with laughter, he would have diagnosed that she still had to work on that area of her belief system.

When working with a bereaved adult, a counselor can assess the patient's progress by his or her use of humor and laughter. At the beginning of an 8-week bereavement group, a 50 year-old gentleman shared details about his wife's death. As he started to share, he started to cry. The third week, the man told the group that he was diagnosed with manic-depression and was on medication. He rarely smiled, and he easily broke into tears. That 8-week session ended without much change in this man's affect. The counselors were concerned about him and, even though they knew he was under psychiatric care, they listened carefully for potential suicidal ideation. He requested to return for the next 8-week session. About halfway through the second session, the man began to smile and started kidding around with the counselors and some of the other members of the group. Although he still had bouts of depression, the depressive symptoms began to decrease. During the third 8-week session he attended, he started laughing and initiating funny stories. At this point, the counselors became more relaxed concerning his potential for suicidal ideation. The man's increased use of humor informed the counselors that the worst of the grief reaction had been worked through. The counselors felt that the gentleman's use of humor was appropriate and not being used to hide or suppress his feelings.

HUMOR AS TREATMENT

Humor "can promote insight by making conscious repressed material, resolving paradoxes, tempering aggression, and revealing new options" and it is a "socially acceptable form of sublimation" (Stuart & Sundeen, 1995, p. 44). That sentence sums up the role humor can play in treating mental illnesses. The rest of this section looks at the therapeutic value of humor as a treatment modality. Remember that humor is only one aspect of interactive care for mentally and emotionally distressed people.

Stuart and Sundeen (1995) cite 14 functions that humor serves within the nurse-patient relationship:

- establishes relationships

- decreases stress and tension

- promotes social closeness
- provides social control
- helps cognitive reframing
- reflects social change
- provides perspective
- expresses emotion
- facilitates learning
- reinforces self-concept
- voices social conflict
- assists with conflict avoidance
- facilitates enculturation
- instills hope.

Stuart and Sundeen (1995) also offer guidelines for the use of humor in the therapeutic milieu. They mention three main occasions when humor may be of therapeutic value, as well as the corresponding times when humor might be inappropriate (see Table 8-1).

It is important to understand how humor can be used in a therapeutic relationship. First of all, humor builds relationships. It helps to establish rapport and can increase communication in a nonthreatening manner. In order for therapy to be effective in the psychiatric arena, the healthcare provider must build a relationship with the patient. Humor can be used as a base on which to build a nurse-patient relationship. The nurse can use this base to respond to the patient

in a way that facilitates growth (Sultanoff, 1992). If not used judiciously, humor can also hurt and destroy relationships.

Humor can also help catch a patient's attention and make messages more likely to be heard (Sultanoff, 1992). It can play a part in establishing and maintaining easier interaction between a patient and an analyst (Robinson, 1991). Sultanoff (1992) suggests that nurses and counselors use tools such as cartoons, anecdotes, jokes, puns, signs, and props to help illustrate the message they would like the patient to hear.

Humor can change how we feel. It is hard to experience humor and be depressed at the same time (Sultanoff, 1992). Here is a little experiment on how a smile can change your feelings:

- Make your face have a neutral expression — neither smiling nor frowning. Be aware of any feelings you might have.
- Make your facial expression a frown. Be aware of how you feel.
- Smile. Check out your feelings.

Many people who do this exercise find that they feel "lighter" when they smile. Was this the case for you? If it was, then you can understand the comment that it is hard to be depressed when you are experiencing humor. That does not mean that negative feelings will not return but, for the moment you

TABLE 8-1: GUIDELINES FOR THE USE OF HUMOR IN THE THERAPEUTIC MILIEU	
THERAPEUTIC	**INAPPROPRIATE**
If the patient has mild to moderate levels of anxiety, functions as a tension reducer	If patient has severe or panic levels of anxiety
When helping patient cope more effectively, improving learning, putting life situations into perspective, and decreasing social distance Understood by the patient for its therapeutic value	If it promotes maladaptive coping, masks feelings, increases social distance, or assists in avoidance of difficult situations
If it is consistent with social and cultural values of the patient, allows the patient to laugh at life, the human situation, or stressors	If it violates the patient's values, ridicules people, or belittles others
(Stuart & Sundeen, 1995, p. 43)	

feel lighter. For psychiatric patients, depressed patients in particular, humor might offer a ray of hope that they could feel better, that they are not stuck in their depression.

Humor may also help reduce performance anxiety. For example, ask a patient to imagine a situation in which he or she experienced humor (Sultanoff, 1992). The patient can then learn to recall this situation when having an anxiety attack. This method helps reduce anxiety by substituting another feeling and by distracting the person from anxiety-producing thoughts.

How a person interprets events has a great impact on how that individual feels. The same set of events can elicit different feelings from different people. Humor can help change a person's thoughts about certain events, thereby changing his or her feelings (Sultanoff, 1992). Humor changes perceptions, and the change in perception alters feelings.

Personal Insight

While recovering from breast surgery, my husband and I were in California on a minivacation. I had developed an infection in the breast area that meant packing the wound with iodoform and changing dressings twice per day. It was a narrow, but deep wound. We had gone for a walk along a marsh area and suddenly my husband stopped and said, "I have to tell you something. It really bothers me to have to pack that wound, so I decided I needed to do something to personalize it. I thought about it and decided that packing the wound was like packing a flint lock musket, so I'm going to call it "flint." We both laughed and later we found that talking about "packing flint" made the dressing changes easier to deal with. Being able to laugh about it changed our perspective from something that was difficult to something that was bearable.

How people behave is linked to how they feel. As previously noted, humor can change the way a per-

son feels; therefore it stands to reason that humor can change the way a person responds. Humor can help lighten a situation and encourage a person to try new things, take risks, and be open to possibilities (Sutlanoff, 1992). When a nurse works with patients who have mental illnesses, a sign of improvement for the mentally ill is the willingness to take risks and try new ways of thinking and behaving.

Research shows that major depression alters immunity by decreasing natural killer (NK) cells (Bauer, Gauer, Luz, Silveira, Nardi, & von Muhlen, 1995; Schleifer, Keller, Bartlett, Eckholdt, & Delaney, 1996;). NK cells assist in the prevention of cancer and viruses. Berk and Tan (1989, cited in Wooten, 1996) discovered that NK cells increase in response to laughter. In addition, studies indicate humor's potential for improving certain immune functions, such as IgA and IgG production. Humor that leads to laughter can help a person feel better physically. These changes all lead up to biochemical changes that can be beneficial for psychiatric patients.

Martin and Lefcourt (1983, cited in Labott, Ahleman, Wolever, & Martin, 1990) report that, as negative life events increase, people who use humor to cope report fewer mood disturbances than individuals who are less likely to use humor. Labott et al. (1990) also discovered that using humor to cope was associated with more positive moods. Furthermore, laughter has positive effects on the cardiovascular, muscular, and skeletal systems.

To use humor therapeutically, guidelines are important. Sultanoff (1994) believes it is important to look at the target of the humor (self, situations, or others); the environmental conditions in which humor is presented (with whom, at what time, and in what setting); and the specific person's receptivity to humor (what type of humor is the person comfortable with, what role does it play in his or her life, is the person able to laugh at himself or herself, and how does the person respond to the humor of others). Pasquali (1995) talks about assessing timing (is this a good time for the client or are they in crisis mode); style (what type of humor is appropriate — joke telling, puns, slapstick, gallows, or funny stories and can they understand a particular style of humor); and context (similar to environmental conditions, this looks at the appropriateness of who, when, and what setting).

Haig (1988) conducted extensive research on the use of humor with different therapeutic approaches. He found that humor played a part in a number of different types of therapy. Humor has been used in behavior therapy, logotherapy, cognitive therapy, family and marital therapies, and group and milieu therapies.

HUMOR IN WORKING WITH THE CHRONICALLY MENTALLY ILL

Pasquali (1995) talks about the use of humor with chronically mentally ill (CMI) patients. Chronic mental illness can lead to defeating feelings and behaviors in both patients and nurses. Mental illness can be a long-term problem with multiple challenges. The problems are not only emotional but also spiritual and social. Isolation of CMI patients is not uncommon. The chronicity of their problems can lead to frustration and feelings of hopelessness and helplessness for both patients and nurses. Incorporating humor therapy may help improve CMI patients' quality of life and provide a model that can help them function in the world (Pasquali, 1995).

Minden (2002) conducted a qualitative study on the effects of a humor group on patients who were forensic psychiatric patients. These patients had committed such crimes as robbery, forgery, assault, arson, rape, incest, and murder. Their psychiatric disorders included anxiety disorder, impulse control disorder, mood disorder, sexual disorders, and schizophrenia. Many of the patients had been or would be institutionalized for years. They tended to feel angry, helpless, and hopeless. Nursing students were used to facilitate the group with the support and guidance of their clinical instructor.

Rules for the humor group were established. Introductions were conducted at each group due to patient turnover. The introductions set the tone by being conducted in a playful manner. Then, a call for jokes was made, which invited patients to share jokes that they knew as a way of sharing humor and preparing for more spontaneous humor. Humorous activities were also planned and sometimes involved patients and students working together. These activities included unique games, songs, dances, skits, or relays for which cooperation was emphasized. The sessions lasted an hour and often closed with talking about a funny group incident, another joke, or a goofy handshake.

After the experience, select members of the group were interviewed. The interviewees reported perceived benefits in their physical (46%), mental (100%), social (77%), and spiritual (46%) health (Minden, 2002). This group had deficits in their mental and social functioning. Minden (2002) notes that, in light of these deficits, "it is encouraging that so many found the group to have significant effects in these areas" (p. 81). One participant indicated that humor made the experience of a group appear less confrontational. "Humor made it easier to hear the feedback because I didn't feel like I was being attacked" (Minden, 2002, p. 82). This humor group intervention acknowledges that humor can be an effective addition to other types of therapy.

Gelkopf, Sigal, and Kramer (1994) studied the use of passive communal laughter to improve social support for a group of inpatients with chronic schizophrenia. The experiment was based on the theory that humor acts to relieve social fear and that laughing with others forms a more integrated psychological unit, increases group cohesiveness, establishes group membership, and relieves group tension. The researchers used humor videos with the experimental group and a combination of humor, romance, action, adventure, drama, and family films with the control group. The results of the study indicate that there was a perceived increase in support from the staff but not from fellow patients (Gelkopt et al., 1994). The researchers were unsure of the reason for the results; however, they noted that the introduction of laughter-stimulating videos appeared to change the social aspects between patients and staff. This did not occur with the control group. It would be interesting to see what would have happened if there was more interaction among the patients, as there had been in the study by Minden (2002).

APPROPRIATE HUMOR

Using humor in the psychiatric setting requires a more cautious approach than in the medical-surgical setting. Although the pointers offered in this section can apply to any patient experiencing the stress of illness, examples have been included to illustrate how they can be applied appropriately in the therapeutic environment for patients with mental disorders.

Darby (1996) offers five areas to assess to determine the type of humor that might be appreciated and effective for a particular patient: (1) attention span, (2) information access, (3) social cues processing, (4) decision making, and (5) focus.

Attention Span

Individuals with mental illness are likely to have short attention spans. These patients can concentrate on a single goal for a brief period of time and then quickly lose interest or divert to another thought or activity. Disease entities that seem to be characterized by the shortest attention spans are:

- Major depression — patients have difficulty concentrating and their thought processes are slowed

- Mania — patients commonly suffer from excessive activity, loose association, and flight of ideas, making concentration difficult

- Schizophrenia (depending on type and severity) — can cause people to have difficulty concentrating on what someone is saying to them; disorganized thinking may make following information difficult

- Attention deficit disorder.

For individuals with short attention spans, humor that has a short buildup would work best. The information presented needs to be delivered quickly. Spontaneous humor might be best for patients who demonstrate difficulty concentrating on information.

The following example illustrates the use of humor for someone with a short attention span:

A depressed patient with PTSD had been coming to group for a few weeks. She had demonstrated improved mood, but one week she came to the group feeling depressed. She stated that everyone was against her. Rather than responding in a way that indicated that the group members were not against her, the leader looked at her and said, "You're right, especially all of us here." She looked at the leader for a few seconds, and burst into laughter, acknowledging that she realized the all or nothing reaction she had was not valid.

Information Input

Individuals experiencing good mental health are usually able to process different pieces of information at once. As an example, a nurse notices that people are gathering outside a patient's room. One person is crying, another is pacing, and another is standing and twisting a cloth in his hand. There is a sense of tension from the three people. The nurse may look at this scene and, through her visual, auditory, and kinesthetic senses, decide that something either is happening or has happened with the patient to cause the people outside the room to be upset. A patient suffering from a thought disorder, would be unable to put this much information together.

Rather, the patient may experience information overload, which may lead to a high-anxiety state.

When using humor with a patient who is mentally ill, it is important to assess how many and which channels of information work. The nurse needs to know if the patient is better able to understand auditory, visual, or kinesthetic cues. Being observant and aware of how a patient learns information and responds to his environment should let the nurse know what avenue of humor the patient may be able to understand best. Patients who learn best with auditory stimuli would understand spoken jokes or humorous statements best. Those patients who learn best visually would be more likely to understand written or visual humor. Patients who are kinesthetic might need someone to act out the joke or humorous information.

Social Cues Processing

Patients who are mentally ill sometimes have difficulty understanding social cues. Some patients may be able to understand abstract thought, but others are concrete thinkers. A concrete thinker, when asked what brought him to the hospital might say, "A taxi." Paranoid individuals are sure everyone is out to get them. For these people, implicit information needs to be made explicit. Darby (1996) demonstrates how to use humor with paranoid patients:

It was April Fool's week. Darby was working the night shift on an inpatient unit. A group of patients wanted to play as many practical jokes on the night shift as they possibly could. The night shift would respond in kind.

One of the patients was paranoid, and he watched what was going on with a rather tense look about him. Darby came up to the patient and asked, "How are things going, John?" The patient said, "I don't know what is going on, but I know that you guys are making fun of me."

At this point, Darby realized that he needed to defuse the patient's anxiety, so he took time to explain about April Fool's Day and attempted to teach him about the customs of that day. He took the implicit social cues and made them explicit through explanation.

After this explanation, John indicated he would like to be involved. He asked to have newspaper placed over his doorframe. When he woke up the next morning and saw his door covered with paper, he reacted as if he were completely surprised. He exhibited a joy much like a 6-year-old.

For someone who has difficulty perceiving social cues, the cues might need to be made explicit. Doing so in a way that does not ruin the punch line would allow an element of surprise. That element of surprise is what leads to something being humorous.

Decision Making

When trying to determine how a person understands and utilizes humor, it is important to assess the person's ability to make decisions. Patients who have difficulty making decisions have difficulty with too many variables. They can process information better with fewer variables. Understanding information or jokes is easier if they are presented in a simple manner. One way to assess a patient's ability to make decisions is to observe how he or she accomplishes tasks of daily living, such as deciding what to wear.

When using humor with patients who have difficulty making decisions, choose humor that requires fewer steps in understanding. Simple cartoons require less processing of information than something as complex as a comedy film (Darby, 1996).

Focus

Some people can see the world in all of its beauty — the blueness of the sky, the flowers in bloom, the birds flying by. Others see the world through what Darby (1996) calls a "telephoto lens" (p.85). A suicidal patient may be so focused on suicide as a means of relieving his emotional pain that he does not see the other options. Darby (1996) shares a story about a young man with obsessive-compulsive disorder. The patient was having difficulty controlling his compulsive need to count to 999 by threes. Using humor, Darby was able to help the patient take himself less seriously. Humor helped him to expand his focus and break his cycle. "If someone is focusing on a small portion of the world to the exclusion of everything else, humor should be directed toward expanding the focus of the individual" (Darby, 1996, p. 53).

Pasquali (1995) offers guidelines nurses need to consider when introducing humor to patients who are chronically mentally ill:

- Realize that clients may use humor to make an uncomfortable situation seem less fearful and anxiety producing.

- Be aware of the amount of smiling and laughing the client engages in.

- Be open to silly and playful thoughts.

- Look for the absurdity in situations or recognize the incongruities.

- Laugh at incongruities in behaviors or situations, never at patient symptoms.

- Start by laughing at yourself.

- Look for opportunities to make others laugh.

- Look for the sunny side of life to develop your sense of humor. You do not have to tell jokes or be a comedian.

The guidelines presented above are intended for patients with mental health problems, but they can be used with other patients as well. Patients who are going through a crisis have a narrow focus, and may have difficulty making decisions, and may only be able to process one piece of information at a time. As important as it is to assess a mental health patient, it is just as important to assess any patient. Humor used inappropriately can be hurtful and damaging to the nurse-patient relationship.

INAPPROPRIATE HUMOR IN THE MENTAL HEALTH SETTING

Because of the difficulties psychiatric patients may have in processing information and their potential for misinterpreting humor, it is important to be aware of when and what type of humor might be inappropriate. The controversy over using humor in therapy arose out of concern for its misuse; therefore, it is important to be aware of what would constitute misuse. Humor should not be used under the following circumstances:

- when the nurse uses it as a defense against his or her own anxieties

- when the nurse uses it as a means of expressing his or her own hostility

- when it is used as a means of ingratiating the nurse with the group

- when there is confusion regarding whether the nurse is serious or joking.

- when it is used indiscriminately without considering the impact on the patient

- when it belittles the patient

- when it is used as a screen to avoid therapeutic intimacy

- if the patient has severe or panic anxiety levels

- if it encourages maladaptive coping responses, covers up feelings, increases social distancing, or helps the patient avoid dealing with difficult situations

- when it violates someone's values.

(Robinson, 1991; Stuart & Sundeen, 1995)

EXAMPLES OF HUMOR USES IN MENTAL HEALTH

A 4-year-old boy shared jokes with his therapist as a way to diffuse the things he feared and to handle inner conflicts. The humor was mutually enjoyed. The young boy's teasing of the therapist seemed to represent a form of finding behavior that let him re-experience separation and reunion over and over (Haig, 1988).

A behavior therapist was working with a 21-year-old woman who was anxious because she was going to attend a banquet where she would meet her ex-boyfriend and his new girlfriend. The therapist employed systematic desensitization with the hope of decreasing her anxiety. Because there was not enough time for the patient to learn systematic relaxation, a humorous vision of her ex-boyfriend in leotards was used as she visualized herself at the banquet. This vision amused her and the evening went off well (Haig, 1988).

"A man with a repeated compulsion for checking the door at night was asked by his therapist to see how many times he could check the door in order to set a new record" (Haig, 1988, p. 146). The patient initially thought this was silly, but 3 days later the compulsion had disappeared.

SUMMARY

Despite the controversy that exists concerning the use of humor in caring for patients who have mental illness, when used with sensitivity and knowledge, humor can be an adjunct to regular psychiatric care. This chapter has reviewed appropriate and inappropriate uses of humor in the therapeutic environment. In the psychiatric arena, as in other areas of healthcare, knowing when and how to use humor is essential.

EXAM QUESTIONS

CHAPTER 8
Questions 64-72

64. There are many reasons for the controversy over the use of humor in the psychiatric setting. Robinson (1991) attributes the cause of this modern controversy to

    a. a psychiatrist's own discomfort with the use of humor.
    b. the stereotypical belief that psychiatric patients are unable to appreciate humor.
    c. Freud's concentration on hostile wit rather than the postive aspects of humor.
    d. the proven lack of therapeutic effect humor has in this setting.

65. Humor can be used in a diagnostic manner with psychiatric patients to

    a. diagnose the type of illness.
    b. assess for signs of psychological improvement.
    c. categorize the degree of impairment.
    d. label the disease process according to the *DSM-IV*.

66. One of the most important uses of humor in the psychiatric setting is as a

    a. means for the patient to poke fun at his illness.
    b. method of promoting insight.
    c. method of developing rapport with patients.
    d. means of facing reality.

67. Inappropriate laughter occurs in the diagnosis of

    a. borderline personality disorder.
    b. bipolar-depressive type.
    c. schizophrenia–disorganized type.
    d. clinical depression.

68. Humor, when used by the nurse, is inappropriate when

    a. puns are used.
    b. humerous props are used.
    c. it prevents dealing with anxieties.
    d. it attempts to change others' perspectives.

69. According to Stuart and Sundeen (1995), the use of humor in a therapeutic milieu is considered appropriate when it

    a. ridicules people and violates their values.
    b. puts life situations into perspective.
    c. promotes social distance from one another.
    d. assists in avoiding difficult situations.

70. Humor is non therapeutic when

    a. used with patients who have mild-moderate levels of anxiety.
    b. used as a means of helping patients cope effectively.
    c. it allows patients to laugh at life.
    d. it masks one's true feelings.

71. When determining which type of humor to use with a patient, Darby suggests assessing

    a. attention span, information access, social cues processing, decision making, and focus.

    b. attention span, information access, favorite sitcom, focus, and social cues processing.

    c. information access, laugh triggers, social cues processing, decision making, and focus.

    d. attention span, information access, affect, decision making, and social cues processing.

72. When planning humor interventions, anticipate a short attention span in patients with

    a. obsessive-compulsive disorder.

    b. narcissistic personality disorder.

    c. somatoform disorder.

    d. mania.

CHAPTER 9

HUMOR AND LEARNING

CHAPTER OBJECTIVES

After completing this chapter, the reader will be able to discuss the ways in which humor can be used in educational situations.

LEARNING OBJECTIVES

After studying this chapter, the reader will be able to

1. describe the effects of humor on learning.

2. differentiate between positive and negative types of humor in learning.

3. demonstrate an understanding of learning theories.

4. describe the effects of aging on learning.

5. discuss ways in which humor can effectively be incorporated into healthcare education.

INTRODUCTION

People rarely succeed unless they have fun in what they are doing.
                                    Dale Carnegie

For many people, the times when they have most enjoyed learning — and often the times when they have learned the most — are when instructors have interjected humor or used exercises to make learning fun. There was a time when people commonly believed that teachers needed to be very seri-

ous because learning was considered a serious business. However, we now know that having fun when you learn helps increase the ability to learn and retain information. This chapter discusses theories about how people learn, presents research on the importance of humor in education, talks about the use of humor in healthcare and patient education, and offers a few examples.

WHY HUMOR?

When trying to learn new material, tension can be a hindrance. When people are upset, anxious, or concerned about something, learning new material can be very difficult. They may find it is easier to focus on the problem rather than the solution. In order for a student to be able to concentrate and learn new information, some form of relaxation on the part of the teacher is important. For example, if a nurse is trying to teach a patient with diabetes, and the patient has a fear of needles, the patient may not hear anything the nurse says. It has been found that humor in the classroom assists in increasing motivation, reducing tension, and aiding in instruction (Flowers, 2001). If this can happen in the classroom, it can likely happen during patient education as well, whether that education is one-on-one or in a group.

Research also shows increased retention of information when humor is used in teaching (Kaplan & Pascoe, 1977; Lamp, 1992). One strategy that has been used to educate postpartum parents about the reality of adapting to a new baby is "Fredricka, A New Mother's Worst Nightmare" (Lamp, 1992).

Fredricka visits postpartum patients on their day of discharge dressed in a manner that humorously depicts the disheveled, fatigued new mother. She appears in a tousled wig with curlers, a bath robe, slippers, dark circles under her eyes, a laundry basket filled with linen, and a toddler-sized doll attached and clinging at knee-level to the robe. She discusses such issues as fatigue, role transition, sibling rivalry, self-image, involution, breast changes, sexual intercourse, the hormonal influences on emotions, and nutrition.

Patients were quite attentive to this humorous approach. Lamp (1992) noted that the information taught was retained and transcended cultural, development, socioeconomic, and educational boundaries.

Humor also seems to increase the ability to think creatively. A study by Isen, Daubman, and Nowicki (1987) demonstrated that people exposed to a few minutes of a comedy film performed better on a problem-solving task than a control group that was not exposed to comedy. Humor may have a positive effect on people, causing them to improve their problem-solving performance. Humor may also play a role in assisting students to make new discoveries and better, more creative decisions.

Robinson (1991) states, "the concepts of creativity and change are closely related to each other as well as to humor and learning" (p. 119). The goal of education is to facilitate change and learning. Creativity, which includes the use of humor, can lead to change. For the educator, it can lead to a change in the methods used for presentation. For the learner, it can assist in the process of understanding and moving toward change.

HUMOR'S ROLE IN LEARNING

In addition to reducing tension, humor helps make concepts that might be difficult easier to under-stand and retain (Bartlett, 2003). As noted by *Humor Project* creator Joel Goodman (n.d.), humor helps the learner go from "HaHa" to "aHa!" Humor captures the learner's attention and holds that attention, increasing the person's motivation and interest in learning. If the person is interested in learning, the information is more likely to be retained. However, this theory is controversial.

Whisonant (1998) notes that a number of studies did not show improved retention with the use of humor. Most of these studies were done in one day. This finding held true even in studies in which posttests were given one week later. However, a study by Kaplan and Pascoe (1977) showed that, although the participants had no immediate effects on retention, there was significantly more effective retention of information for those participants who viewed humorous items than those who viewed nonhumorous items when they took a posttest six weeks later.

A study reported by Delp and Jones in 1996 (cited in Schrecengost, 2001) explored the effects of cartoons on patient comprehension of and compliance with wound care instructions. The study involved 234 patients who presented to the emergency room with simple lacerations. The experimental group received instructions that contained cartoons, and the control group received instructions without cartoons. The patients in the experimental group were more likely to have read the discharge instructions, more likely to answer all the wound care questions correctly, and more compliant with wound care. This study indicates that cartoon illustrations can be an effective teaching tool and may improve patient compliance with emergency room wound care instructions.

Schrecengost (2001) studied the effects of humor on postoperative teaching among 50 patients who were scheduled to undergo coronary artery bypass graft or valve surgery. All the patients were given a pretest. Then they were presented with a patient-teaching booklet. The experimental group received a booklet with cartoons representing three postoperative exercises. The control group's booklet did not contain cartoons. Both booklets contained the same information. The results of this study indicate that both groups had improved knowledge. Although there was no statistically significant difference in knowledge, the experimental group did slightly better on the posttest. It would have been interesting to know if the experimental group found the reading of the information more enjoyable than the control group did.

Humor also assists in increasing a student's self-esteem, sense of empowerment, and confidence in being able to learn the material (Berk, 2002). Humor has been found to help increase problem solving and performance on recognition tasks and spatial temporal reasoning. Schrecengost (2001) reminds us that humor should not replace other teaching methods, but it can work to reinforce or strengthen the information offered. Berk (2002) contends that, if nothing else, humor gives the learner the ability to endure sitting through the lesson.

LEARNING THEORIES

Incorporating effective, appropriate humor into teaching is easier when the educator understands how people learn. This section presents information that may be useful in assisting nurses to comfortably add humor to their patient-teaching styles. Malouf (2003) states that teaching is a skill. The best way to develop a skill is to understand the underlying process and to practice. To understand how to be an effective teacher, it is important to understand theories of how people learn.

Overview of Learning Theories

How people gather, process, remember, and use information has captured the interest of philosophers, psychologists, and various other individuals for years. As a result, there are many learning theories. A few of these theories are discussed here.

Bower and Hilgard (1981) note that there are basically two opposing positions on how knowledge is acquired: *empiricism* and *rationalism*. Those who subscribe to the empiricism theory believe that all knowledge evolves through sensory experience. They believe that all complex ideas come from a basic stock of simple ideas, and complex ideas can be reduced to these simple ideas. Empiricism theorists also believe that ideas are connected through association of experiences occurring closely together in time and that the mind is like a machine with no mysterious components. Empiricists allege that the degree of association (memory) varies in direct proportion to the vividness, frequency, duration, and timing of the experience.

Rationalism, in contrast, involves the belief that reason is the main source of knowledge. It is reason, rather than data obtained through sensory experience, that is the basis of knowledge. Rationalists see data as unstructured, undifferentiated chaos that provides raw material to an interpretive mechanism. This interpretive mechanism uses the raw data as clues to the probable source and meaning of the material (Bower and Hilgard, 1981). Descartes, Kant, and other rationalists believed that relationships between basic sense points were as primary and psychologically intense as the sense points themselves. As an example, when we listen to music, we do not hear just the tones, but coherent melody (Bower and Hilgard, 1981). When we hear a joke, it is the recognition of the incongruity that allows us to "get it."

Empiricism and rationalism provide the background for more modern learning theories. Pavlov and Skinner, who subscribed to the empiricism theory, are two of the names most commonly connected with the *stimulus response theory*. Many individuals are familiar with the story of Pavlov and his dog, in which the stimulus of a ringing bell cause the dog to salivate even if no food was presented. According to this theory, learning takes place when a stimulus represents an event. The ringing of the bell represents the presentation of food. Eventually, the animal or person responds in a predictable manner (salivation) without the presentation of the reward (food).

Skinner's theory of learning also deals with behavior responses. He believed that learned behavior affected subsequent behaviors (Dworetzky & Davis, 1989; Hergenhahn, 1990; Murphy, 1978). This theory is known as *operant conditioning*. For example, if a young child played with a television set and was told "no" often enough, the child would learn that the television was not something with which to play. Or, in the field of humor, if a child is told that being silly is not proper behavior, he or she learns that actions others might find silly, but he or she finds enjoyable, are not okay. Positive reinforcement of behavior is more likely to result in repetition of that behavior (Hergenhahn, 1990).

Arguments against Skinner's theory focus on the concept of cause and effect. However, for many years, Skinner's principles have been used in schools. Students are rewarded (behavior reinforcement) for doing well in class by such methods as positive affirmations, high grades, and praise. Students begin to recognize that parcels of knowledge can be applied to other situations. Although more information on how learning takes place has become available over the years, some of the operant conditioning principles are still applicable today.

One part of operant conditioning that might be a concern in educating others is that children are taught that education is serious — that clowning around when you are supposed to be learning is not appropriate. This conditioning can have a negative effect because the child may not recognize that use of humor and play does not mean that the teacher of the material should not be taken seriously. Research has demonstrated that some material is retained more effectively if humor and play are used in teaching (Berk, 2002; Goodman, n.d.; Kaplan & Pascoe, 1977). Learning may be serious business, but that does not mean it cannot be fun.

Learning also takes place through observation of the behaviors of others. Using research on the influences of social behavior, Albert Bandura pioneered the *social learning theory* (Murphy, 1978). Bandura (1997) states that individuals hold beliefs that allow them to exercise a measure of control over their feelings, thoughts, and actions. He notes that behavior is influenced by what people think, feel, and believe. Behavior is the result of the interplay between the individual's personal self-system and external sources of influence (Hergenhahn, 1990; Pajares, 1997). The self-system encompasses self-concept, self-esteem, and values.

Social cognitive theory assumes:

- reciprocal interactions exist between individuals, behaviors, and the environment

- learning can be enactive and vicarious

- maturation and experience increase a person's knowledge

- there is a distinction between learning and performance

The term *reciprocal interactions* refers to interacting environmental variables, behaviors, and personal factors, such as the person's analysis of the situation (Hergenhahn, 1990; Schunk, 1991). The interaction between the person and the environment is considered highly complex and individualized. Each individual brings to a situation remnants of previous experiences that are employed in the present situation. How events turn out in the present situation will, in turn, help determine the response in the next situation (Hergenhahn, 1990).

Enactive learning takes place when a person learns from his or her own actions. *Vicarious learning* takes place by listening to or observing others or by reading. For example, a nurse can teach a patient how to perform a procedure such as insulin injection by demonstrating the procedure and then having the patient demonstrate the procedure back to the nurse. Or, the patient can read about preventative measures and evaluate the results of their learning by discussing what they understood and receiving feedback from the nurse and others.

Another assumption of social cognitive theory is the distinction made between learning and performance of previously learned behaviors (Schunk, 1991). Knowledge may be acquired but not demonstrated at the time of learning. Social cognitive theory outlines three types of knowledge: declarative, procedural, and conditional. Declarative knowledge encompasses facts, scripts, and organized passages. *Scripts* refer to concepts such as the events of a story. Words of a song demonstrate the concept of organized passages. Concepts, rules, and algorithms are examples of procedural knowledge. Conditional knowledge refers to "knowing when to employ forms of declarative and procedural knowledge and why it is important to do so" (Schunk, 1991, p. 104).

Much of the time, declarative, procedural, and conditional knowledge interact (Schunk, 1991). For example, during a lecture, participants think about what is being presented (environment influences cognition). Participants who do not understand ask questions about the presentation (conditions influence behavior). The presenter responds to the question (behavior influences environment). The presenter asks the participants to engage in an experiential experience (environment influences cognitions, which influence behavior). The participants enjoy the activity and request more time to experience the results, and the presenter grants the time (cognitions influence behavior, which influences environment).

Modeling is a social theory concept that refers to behavioral, cognitive, and affective changes that occur after observing one or more models (Schunk, 1991). Bandura (cited in Schunk, 1991) concluded that modeling serves functions of inhibition and disinhibition, response facilitation, and observational learning. Observing a model is believed to strengthen or weaken inhibitions over previously learned behaviors. The responses of others to a situation can facilitate behavior in others. An example of this

behavior is someone laughing at an event and then causing others around to start laughing. Observational learning occurs when observers take on behaviors that are new and have been modeled by others. An example of observational learning is if someone at a humor program notices others around him being playful and, although it may be out of character, tries the playful behaviors to see how it feels.

Modeling can also take place when a nurse laughs at herself for a mistake that she made, such as mispronouncing a word. This response can also help to reduce stress. Stress relief can be further demonstrated by asking the patient to join in a laughing exercise. If the nurse starts to laugh, the patient will most likely follow the example because laughter tends to be contagious. After the laughter exercise, the patient can then be asked to describe what he or she felt, and the nurse can build on that sharing to talk about the ways laughter and humor can help decrease tension and change the perspective of a situation.

Modeling involves four subprocesses: attention, retention, production, and motivation (Hergenhahn, 1990; Kearsley, 1997; Schunk, 1991). *Attention* refers to things a person notices about his or her environment. Information that is likely to catch a person's attention can vary, depending on a number of factors, such as movement, color, sound, or location (Berk, 2002). People are most likely to attend to things or events they perceive to be valuable (Hergenhahn, 1990; Kearsley, 1997).

Retention is the storage of information and includes the ability to recall what has been coded, cognitively organized, symbolically rehearsed, or rehearsed through movement or physical manipulation (Hergenhahn, 1990; Kearsley, 1997; Schunk, 1991). Colorful cartoons, humorous songs, and specific movements tend to hold people's attention and increase retention (Berk, 2002).

Production refers to reproducing modeled events into overt behaviors. This process occurs when patients or students demonstrate that they have learned a skill or information that has been modeled. By practicing the skills learned and receiving feedback, the learner can refine their knowledge and perform skills more accurately (Schunk, 1991).

Motivation may be either intrinsic or extrinsic (Huitt, 2001). In other words, motivation may occur through the external environment by viewing behaviors of others, or by the expectations of others, or it may be self-motivated or internal. According to social learning theory, reinforcement, either direct (experiencing their own consequences for behavior) or vicarious (seeing how others have consequences applied to their behaviors) provides the motivation for action (Hergenhahn, 1990; Huitt, 2001). Individuals are more likely to be motivated to adopt behaviors if the behaviors result in outcomes they value (Hergenhahn, 1990; Kearsley, 1997). Humor is a positive means of reinforcing the information and may increase the motivation to continue learning.

Social learning theory recognizes that individuals develop performance standards by which they evaluate their own behavior. They maintain this behavior through self-regulation (Hergenhahn, 1990). *Self-efficacy* is an important variable in determining self-regulatory behavior (Hergenhahn, 1990). According to Bandura (1997), self-efficacy is a belief in one's ability to organize and implement actions necessary to reach designated performance levels. Individuals who do not see that they have the ability to succeed can, through verbal persuasion from others, be encouraged and supported to reach their goals and to make the effort to succeed.

According to Kearsley (1997), the main principles of Bandura's social learning theory are as follows:

* Organizing and rehearsing modeled behavior symbolically and then performing it overtly will result in the highest level of observational learning. By coding modeled behavior into images,

labels, or words, better retention will occur than with observation alone.

* Modeled behavior is more likely to be adopted by an individual if the outcome is something of value.

* A modeled behavior is more likely to be adopted if the model has admired status and the behavior has functional value.

Adult Learning Theories

Today, it is recognized that adults learn differently from children. Until the 20th century, however, the theoretical framework for all education was *pedagogy* (Knowles, 1978). The literal meaning of the term *pedagogy* is the art and science of teaching children. After World War I, there emerged an increasing notion that adults had unique characteristics as learners (Knowles, 1978). It was recognized that adults enter the learning process with more prior knowledge than children. Adults display increased variability due to experiences, culture, prior learning, and other influences on their knowledge. They also display less plasticity, or moldability, than children (Long, 1990).

Malcolm Knowles, a recognized expert in adult education, uses the term *andragogy* to describe his model of adult learning (Goodboe, 1995; Merriam & Brockett, 1997). Knowles (1978) lists four main assumptions of andragogy:

1. Adults prefer to be self-directed.

2. Adults bring unique life experiences with them to the learning situation. These experiences can be used as a resource for learning.

3. Adults' willingness to learn is usually linked to what adults consider relevant. It is believed that adults will learn faster and with more lasting results if the material is significant to them and to their present lives (Vella, 1994).

4. Adults' orientation to learning is problem-centered (Knowles, 1978). Adults tend to seek out learning because they have use for the

knowledge or the skill being taught. "Learning is a means to an end, not an end in itself" (Zemke & Zemke, 1984, p. 1).

A number of characteristics specific to adult learners have emerged (Malouf, 2003; Merriam & Brockett, 1997; Taylor & Burgess, 1995). Nurses need to understand how to present material that will meet the expectations and needs of these learners. Table 9-1 depicts adult learner characteristics and points to keep in mind when designing educational programs.

Most adults are self-directed learners. Self-directed learners know what they want to learn and are willing to accept responsibility for discovering the information and resources necessary to meet their needs or desires related to acquisition of that knowledge (Brookfield, 1986; Knowles, 1978). Some researchers define *self-directedness* as a learner's ability to independently plan, conduct, and evaluate his or her own learning experience (Brookfield, 1986). Brookfield (1986) cautions that using the term *self-directed* might indicate that the person is wholly in control of the learning process.

It is important to remember that no individual can undertake the process of learning or education without some external sources or stimuli.

Studies undertaken by Brookfield and others indicate some need for careful utilization of terminology when viewing self-directedness in the light of independent or dependent learning (Brookfield, 1986). Studies of individuals from different cultures indicate that people who score high on self-directedness may prefer dependent learning techniques. A 1984 study by Thiel (as cited in Brookfield, 1986) found that individuals from French-speaking Quebec who were considered self-directed or independent learners because they sought learning outside the formal educational environment preferred learning through information gathered from others over using their own analytical skills. They did well in situations that required them to adapt to specific and immediate situations. Learning through trial and error, or some type of active experimentation in investigating concrete experiences, was preferred.

TABLE 9-1: SUMMARY OF ADULT LEARNER CHARACTERISTICS

Characteristics	Potential Barriers	Approaches
Many prior experiences	Prior experiences might match present knowledge, as can be seen in changes in childrearing practices over the years.	Utilize what learners already know and build on it.
Set habits and strongly established expectations	Habits are easier to make than to break. Learning requires change, and change may be resisted.	In order to facilitate change, make learners feel safe. Humor results in a relaxed atmosphere that can encourage learning.
Many preoccupations	Maintaining attention may be a challenge.	To keep and hold attention, use visuals. Have learners participate in learning. Make it fun.
Attitudes often firmly established	Learning new material, especially if it requires a change in lifestyle, can be difficult.	Make learners understand why new behaviors would be better than the old in order to promote change.
Specific purpose for learning	Learners may feel as if the information to be learned does not apply to them.	Show learners that the learning will satisfy their needs, solve a problem, and be used immediately.

(Knowles, 1978)

The populations studied by Thiel and Brookfield felt that the most important learning resource was watching or listening to other people (Brookfield, 1986). Participants saw peers and fellow learners as providers of information, skill models, and reinforcers of learning, as well as counselors in times of crisis. Brookfield (1986) states, "Successful self-directed learners appear to be highly aware of context in the sense of placing their learning within a social setting in which advice, information, and the skill modeling provided by other learners are crucial conditions for self-directed learning" (p. 44).

Zemke and Zemke (1984) note that adult learners are motivated to learn in order to cope with specific life-changing events, such as marriage, a new job, a promotion, illness, losing a job, or divorce. As the stress of such life changes accumulates, the motivation to cope with these changes through learning increases. Once adults are convinced that change is inevitable, they will participate in any learning that appears to be able to help them cope with the transition (Long, 1990; Zemke & Zemke, 1984).

Long (1990) discusses the above impetus as well as personal growth motives. Some adults participate in learning to become more informed individuals. Others choose learning experiences to meet new and interesting people. Skill acquisition that results in a way to spend spare time more enjoyably, such as skiing or scuba diving, may be the motivation for learning. In other words, there are many motivators for adult learning. These motivators can result in self-directed learning. Finding out what motives stimulate patients to learn can assist in designing patient-education programs.

Wlodkowski (1990) notes that psychologists tend to use the term *motivation* to describe processes that stimulate behavior and give purpose or direction to the behavior. Functions seen as necessary in learning, such as concentration, attention, effort, perseverance, and initiative, can be strongly influenced by a person's internal or external environment.

Wlodkowski (1990) states that these influences make motivation unstable. According to Wlodkowski (1990), factors that help maintain motivation include feeling successful, viewing efforts as worthwhile or valuable, and experiencing pleasure in the learning. Humor can be a motivator in learning (Hudson, 2001; Lomax & Moosavi, 2002).

Grow (1996) mentions that not all adult learners are self-directed. Individuals come to the learning environment at different stages of life development. Students who are accustomed to directive learning feel uncomfortable in a self-directed learning environment. These individuals want and expect the facilitator to be in control of the learning environment. They also expect lecture presentations that allow them to listen, practice, and receive immediate correction. Other learners may enter the learning environment with some desire to be in control of their own learning but need and seek guidance in methods of acquiring information. As students become more self-directed, they tend to desire fewer teacher-directed activities.

Diversity is a key word when thinking about adult learners. Because adults bring to the learning environment different physiological, psychological, and sociological experiences, speaking of an "adult learner" as if there is a generic adult is erroneous (Long, 1990). Adult learners can range in age from 20 to 90. Learning abilities, prior knowledge, physiological issues, and many other factors are involved in determining how and what an adult learner may learn.

Effects of Aging on Learning

As educators, nurses must also consider the needs of older adults. Who is considered an older adult learner? Do older adults continue to be involved with learning? What effects do memory and brain changes have on older adult learning? In what ways do older adults learn differently from younger adults? Some authors refer to individuals ages 50 and older as older adults (Kidd, 1990;

Lumsden, 1987-1988). The Elderhostel program, a program designed for older adults, is available for individuals older than age 55 (Elderhostel Company, n.d.). Kleiman (1995) refers to individuals ages 55 to 65 as *young old*.

As adults age, their interest in education changes and their ability to learn changes. However, change does not necessarily mean a decrease in ability.

Physiological changes that occur with aging can affect the speed of information gathering. Many adults in their 40s begin to develop presbyopia, a condition that requires bifocals, or the use of magnifying devices. Adjustment to these visual assertive devices can increase assimilation difficulty, especially if learning involves the use of print and projected media, requiring the learner to shift fields of vision from 18 inches to 20 feet and then back again (Long, 1990).

Another normal aspect of aging that can affect the learning ability of an individual is impaired hearing. In fact, older learners express concerns about reduced hearing abilities more often than they do about visual problems. One problem related to impaired hearing is a lack of awareness on the part of the learner. Hearing deficits related to age commonly occur insidiously, so the individual may not be aware of the problem. Presbycusis, a hearing defect that involves inability to hear high pitched sounds, leads to misinterpretation of words because certain sounds are harder to discern (Long, 1990).

Another age-related concern is energy expenditure. For some older adults, age brings with it a decrease in energy level. This can lead to increased fatigue that results in decreased attention levels. Long (1990) notes that teachers need to be sensitive to older learners' physical expenditure needs in order to keep them engaged in the learning process. Humor works as a stimulator and, according to Berk (2002), it can "increase the students' mental and physical pain tolerance for sitting through" the class or lesson (p. 60).

Beliefs about cognitive issues in aging can lead to educator bias. Unfortunately, some individuals believe that the ability to learn decreases with age. Although studies indicate that there is some slowing of the cognitive processes with aging (Ferraro, 1997; Knight, 1996), Ferraro (1997) notes that, with normal aging, decline in problem solving was found only among those in their 70s. Knight (1996) discusses that the use of working memory declines with age. Age-related changes could decrease the pace and increase the effort of new learning as well as affect language comprehension. This does not mean, however, that the older adult cannot learn new information; it just means that the presentation of the information may need to be adjusted to meet the needs of older adults. Humorous or playful interactions that remind older learners of their former experiences and tap into their former knowledge may be beneficial in the learning process. Remember, however, that the comprehension of the punch line in jokes may decrease with age (Kingsley, 2003). As the frontal lobe in the brain deteriorates with aging, mental flexibility, the ability to perform abstract reasoning, and working memory may be affected, which may be the reasons for decreased humor comprehension.

Studies indicate that the tendency to attend formal education declines with age. However, informal learning projects seem to increase with age (Lumsden, 1987-88). Lumsden (1987-88) notes that perhaps "at some point during the adult years, there occurs a shift from a preference for institutionally sponsored educational activities to a preference for self-initiated, self-planned, self-directed learning" (p. 11).

McCullough-Brabson (1995), a music educator who teaches for Elderhostel, discusses her experience with older adult learners. While doing an informal survey, she discovered reasons people attended Elderhostel programs. These reasons included the excitement of the learning experience; an economical way to get good food, comfortable lodging, and well-done programs; a stimulating vacation; and a desire and interest in learning new things. McCullogh-Brabson (1995) shares her ingredients for success with teaching the older adult. She notes that the facilitator needs to know the subject material very well. Organization and preparedness are important. Older adults want an "organizational road map" (p. 42) in the form of a detailed syllabus so that they know the objectives and the plan for each day and class session. She suggests using various methods, such as videos, hands-on experience, and field trips, to illustrate major points. Enthusiasm, animation, and a sense of humor are important characteristics of a good facilitator. It is also important for the facilitator to allow time for comments and questions but to control the class if someone tends to monopolize the session. The need for awareness of the physical needs of older adults is stressed. Facilitators should use visual aids that are large and easy to read. When the facilitator is designing handouts or overheads, it is important to remember that dark words on a light background are easiest to read.

Another physical need that must be considered is the temperature of the room. As adults age, their subcutaneous fat decreases and the body's ability to maintain heat changes. Therefore, the room should be a comfortable temperature for the participants. Most older adults prefer a room that is on the warm side.

ADDING HUMOR TO HEALTHCARE EDUCATION

Now that we have some understanding of how scientists believe people learn, let us explore what can be done to increase learning through humor. The use of humor must be tasteful not hurtful, and it must relate to the topic in order to be meaningful for the adult learner. Whether you are teaching to individuals, groups, or students, incorporating humor can enhance your lessons and improve attention and retention.

Some people are uncomfortable about adding humor to their teaching material because they cannot tell jokes. The ability to tell jokes is not necessary for the addition of humor in an educational session. Using visual aids helps increase understanding, so using cartoons or cartoon-type figures might be one way of adding humor that doesn't involve telling jokes. The idea of using humor is not to put on a show but to find a way that is comfortable for you to interject humor where appropriate (Hudson, 2001).

Another aspect of using humor is being open to it. Be alert to ways of presenting information without putting other people down. If possible, make yourself the object of the humor. Masie (2003) states that the trick to education is for teachers to make sure they do not shut off humor as a tool. A funny presenter does not have to tell funny stories; he or she just needs to connect with common truths that will bring out the humor response (Masie, 2003).

The following example illustrates how to use humor to teach patients about proper alignment following hip surgery:

> Share with the patient that, when cutting up a chicken, to dislocate and remove the thigh at the hip, you bring the chicken's thigh toward it's body and rotate it inward and toward the center, causing the hip to pop. If the patient does not want to be a chicken, he or she needs to be sure to not repeat that action.

If you make a mistake or use the wrong words when explaining something, make light of the situation in some way. Making a comment such as, "my mouth runs faster than my brain" can help to demonstrate in a humorous manner that mistakes happen and are just a part of life. If the nurse can laugh at herself, hopefully the patient will recognize that everyone makes mistakes and, therefore, will not be as anxious about learning new material. Humor is viewed as a way to humanize the relationship between student and teacher (Lawson, 2001).

When providing patient teaching, the nurse needs to be alert to subtle uses of humor by the patient. This humor can provide clues to the patient's anxieties and hopes (Lawson, 2001). A patient's humor usage can also provide clues about financial concerns, family pressures, and fear of failing.

SUGGESTIONS FOR THE NURSE-EDUCATOR

For those who teach nursing or continuing education for nurses, here are a few suggestions for ways to add humor into your educational process. If your job is to design math quizzes for nurses, add a few humorous questions. The following are suggestions by Sue Moore (2002) taken from the web site www.allnurses.com

☺ You are assisting a primary nurse with charcoal administration down an orogastric tube. The room measures 8 ft by 12 ft. The patient starts to retch before the tube is pulled. Knowing that charcoal can spew out of a tube in a 5-ft radius (even with a thumb over the opening) and the stretcher is 2 ft wide, how many feet per second must you back up to get less charcoal on you than the primary nurse?

☺ You were assigned two large treatment rooms and the gynecologic room. By the end of the day, you have cared for ten patients. Four patients were females over the age of 80, all complaining of weakness. Two patients were male, ages 72 and 50. The last four were females, between the ages of 24 and 40, all complaining of abdominal pain. It is 3:00 p.m. and time to restock the rooms. How many bedpans will you need?

☺ You are the primary nurse for an elderly patient with congestive heart failure. The IV stick was exceptionally difficult, but you are able to start an 18-gauge catheter on the second attempt. You leave the room to check on another patient. A relative thinks that the IV has stopped dripping and opens the clamp. How much IV fluid will infuse before you return?

☺ You have been asked to cover a coworker's rooms during her break. One of her patients is an elderly, confused male with an enlarged prostate. A catheter has been inserted and his physician is coming to see him. Somehow he manages to get off the stretcher. The drainage bag is firmly hooked to the side rail. Knowing that the catheter is 16 in. long and the drainage tubing is 3 ft long, will he be able to reach the door before pulling out the catheter?

Do you teach nursing documentation? Are you tired of trying to explain why it is important that the documentation is clear and accurate? Try using examples of what poor documentation can look like. Ask students what they think would happen if the following type of documentation were to be presented in court:

☺ The patient presented with left chest pain. Patient has chest pain if she lies on her left side for over a year.

☺ Healthy appearing decrepit 69-year-old male, mentally alert but forgetful admitted to room 304.

☺ The patient states she is numb from her toes down.

☺ When she fainted, her eyes rolled around the room.

When talking about the importance of patient teaching, one of the messages the instructor hopes the student hears is that it is important to be sure the patient understands the instructions or procedure. This can be accomplished by asking the patient to either demonstrate the procedure or tell you what he or she has heard. To demonstrate this point, share a humorous situation. Here is an example:

A physician seeing a patient in the office found the patient's wound dressing to be extremely loose. When asked why the dressing was so loose, the patient explained, "Well, the nurse told me not to get the bandage wet, so whenever I take a shower, I take it off."

Flournoy, Turner, and Combs (2001) suggest using an interactive bulletin board to increase staff education in a critical care unit. The authors used humor to teach clinical concepts and found that certain components are necessary. First, there must be "a hook." Without something to draw people to the bulletin board, no matter how important the information, it will not be read. Then set up a pathway to follow, starting with the objectives, and create a smooth path with arrows leading to the information. The hook should be the "story line," which introduces the objective for the "lesson." Use a humorous story line by being creative. Perhaps a funny incident relates to the clinical topic. To be sure the story line will be effective, ask the following questions:

☺ Can this be misinterpreted by the participants?

☺ Will this offend participants?

☺ Will it decrease the author's credibility?

☺ Will it distract from the key points?

The second component is characters. Flournoy, Turner, and Combs (2001) suggest using cartoon characters. These can be hand drawn, computer clip art, or newspaper clippings. use three principal characters. "One presents the information, one questions it, and one resists change" (p. 32cc8). The idea of resisting change is an interesting one, because experience shows that nurses may be reluctant to change viewpoints or ways of doing things.

The third component is the addition of diagrams, pathophysiology pictures, or statistical information. Learning requires a number of senses. Varying how the material is presented strengthens the delivery.

The fourth component is the posttest. Posttest questions relate to the clinical topic objectives. Berk (2002) suggests using a little humor in the test questions. Take the following example:

Ibuprofen is the generic drug name for which popular brand name medication?

   a. Advil®

   b. Black & Decker®

   c. Charmin®

   d. Docker®

   e. Exxon®

Here is an example of how Flournoy, Turner, and Combs (2001) presented information on three different methods for obtaining a central venous pressure (CVP) measurement. The background color for the presentation was red because red is a powerful color and attracts attention. Numbered squares were used to indicate the flow of the story line. They used colored, computer-generated cartoon characters that included a reporter, office staff, and discharged patients who were visiting. Interaction between the characters was displayed through the use of call-out bubbles. They designed a story in which the hospital office receives an announcement about three methods to obtain CVP. This announcement puts the office into a state of turmoil. A reporter from the *HitNurse Gazette* covers the story about this change. Through the use of diagrams, another character, named Calm Larry, explains how to implement the change. The story continues with some discussion by the cartoon characters about the need to change the way things are, and Smarty-Pants Mike explains the three methods that can be used. Brief questions are asked by the characters and Smarty-Pants Mike answers them. Then the reporter directs the participants to the posttest envelope. This particular training resulted in an average score of 90%.

THE NEGATIVE SIDE OF HUMOR IN EDUCATION

A discussion of the use of humor for teaching purposes would not be complete without discussing the problems that can occur when humor is used inappropriately. Some people feel that humor has no place in education and may become offended if humor is used in the classroom or in patient education. When using humor, be sensitive to the responses of the student or students. Any humor that puts someone down should not be used. In reality, that is not humor but an insult. As Boerman-Cornell (2000) said, "Humor that hurts the audience is counterproductive" (¶20). Hurtful humor stifles creativity and learner participation and creates an atmosphere of fear.

SUMMARY

Learning is an ongoing process. Many theories address how people learn, however, no one theory covers all the aspects of learning. Individuals learn based on their genetic background, psychological and physical well-being, and the opportunities that they encounter. Developmental issues affect the learning process. Most people become increasingly self-directed as they age. Nurses can assist the learner by being aware of the learner's style, developmental level, innate ability, and recent research in the field of knowledge acquisition.

There is strong evidence that humor has a place in education, whether it be patient education or nursing education. Raseshide (1993, cited in Flowers, 2001) suggests seven guidelines for using humor in the classroom. These guidelines serve as a good summary for humor in education, no matter what the environment.

☺ Be aware of and receptive to the many uses of humor.

☺ Never use humor to ridicule or embarrass the learner.

☺ Humor should serve a specific purpose, even if it is used spontaneously.

☺ Humor should be appropriate to the learner's ability level.

☺ Spontaneous and planned humor should be

used in teaching.

☺ People should laugh at themselves occasionally to demonstrate that they are real people.

☺ Sarcasm should only be used if it is playful, and even then it should be used very carefully. It should be noted that some student's find sarcasm inappropriate and hurtful.

EXAM QUESTIONS

CHAPTER 9
Questions 73-81

73. A nurse plans on teaching her newly diagnosed cardiac patient about potential lifestyle changes necessary to improve his cardiovascular health. She decides to add humor into the teaching process. Adding humor is a way to

   a. decrease tension so that learning is more likely to take place.

   b. increase tension, thereby increasing creativity.

   c. emphasize the importance of lifestyle changes that are necessary.

   d. help patients laugh at themselves.

74. A nurse-manager is planning an inservice session to teach the staff how to use a new IV pump. She designs the program using cartoons and dresses up the IV pole as a clown. This type of approach will probably

   a. cause staff ridicule.

   b. make the administration uncomfortable.

   c. lose the interest of the learner.

   d. increase the interest and attention of the learner.

75. Using cartoons in a preoperative teaching booklet

   a. helps increase comprehension.

   b. always guarantees compliance.

   c. make the booklet more difficult to read.

   d. insults adults and should be avoided.

76. Negative reinforcement of behaviors, such as repeatedly saying "no" or "bad," is an example of

   a. rationalism.

   b. social learning.

   c. inactive learning.

   d. operant conditioning.

77. A nurse is preparing to teach a 76-year-old woman how to administer her own insulin. The most important principle to keep in mind during the instruction is that

   a. older adults cannot learn new information.

   b. humor for an older adult is distracting and should never be used.

   c. using humor is helpful, but complex humor may not be effective.

   d. learning methods do not need to be adjusted for age.

78. To incorporate humor into educational materials, nurses must be able to

   a. tell jokes.

   b. see the funny side of life.

   c. know people who have a good sense of humor.

   d. be sarcastic and hurtful.

79. During a follow-up appointment with his cardiologist, a patient tells the doctor that he is having trouble with one of his "patches." He says, "The nurse told me to put on a new one every 6 hours and now I'm running out of places to put it!" The doctor has the patient undress and discovers what he hoped he would not find. The patient had more than 50 patches on his body.

    This story demonstrates a situation in which

    a. the patient may not have understood the patient-teaching instructions.

    b. the nurse's use of humor was inappropriate.

    c. the patient was just being noncompliant.

    d. the patient made his own decisions about his healthcare.

80. A nurse is demonstrating the use of a new patient assistance device for arthritic patients. Suddenly, he drops the device and it clatters to the floor. The nurse realizes that he needs to break his tension and that of the observers.

    The most appropriate action to lighten the situation would be for the nurse to

    a. pick up and continue as if nothing happened.

    b. ask someone else to pick it up and continue as if nothing happened.

    c. look at his hands, rub them as if trying to get the grease off, and say something about slippery hands.

    d. leave it where it fell and continue on as if nothing happened.

81. A negative type of humor in teaching that should be avoided is

    a. laughing at yourself occasionally.

    b. to ridicule or embarrass the learner.

    c. the use of empathetic humor.

    d. spontaneous humor with a purpose.

CHAPTER 10

DESIGNING HUMOR PROGRAMS IN WORK SETTINGS

CHAPTER OBJECTIVE

After completing this chapter, the reader will be able to discuss different types of formal humor programs and the concerns and considerations related to implementing such a program.

LEARNING OUTCOMES

After studying the chapter, the reader will be able to

1. explain different types of humor projects.

2. design a humor project.

3. create a humor program in his or her facility.

4. discuss the role of caring clowns.

5. explain how someone might become involved in care clowning.

INTRODUCTION

Not only is it important to understand the benefits of humor, it is also important to find ways to add humor to everyday experiences. A number of formal methods can be used to accomplish this, such as the use of humor rooms, humor carts, or humor baskets. Caring clowns is another means of intervention. This chapter explores formal methods of introducing humor into your life and the lives of patients and coworkers.

HUMOR PROJECTS

Commonly used types of humor projects include humor rooms, humor carts, humor baskets, and caring clowns.

Humor Rooms

Humor rooms are rooms where patients, family, friends, and staff can get together to laugh, play, and relax. These rooms are commonly decorated with comfortable furniture, pleasing artwork, and plants. One of the first humor rooms created was "The Lively Room" at DeKalb Hospital in Decatur, Georgia (Wooten, 1996). It was started by Sandra Yates, RN, and W.W. Lively, a hospital board member.

Humor rooms usually contain reading areas, video equipment, and shelves filled with humorous books, videos, audiocassettes, and other materials. If the room is large enough, it can be used as a place for informal gatherings, group sessions, and even birthday parties or weddings.

The negative side of a humor room is that it is stationary. Patients from other areas of a hospital have limited access to it. In addition, it is difficult for patients who are seriously ill or bedridden to access the materials in the room. Humor rooms work well in long-term care facilities, rehabilitation units, psychiatric units, and outpatient clinics (Wooten, 1996).

Humor Carts

Humor carts can be filled with the same materials and supplies as humor rooms. However, carts can be wheeled into a patient's room to brighten the somber, scary, stress-filled days that go along with hospital admissions. In 1989, Leslie Gibson, RN, created one of the first humor carts at Morton Plant Hospital in Clearwater, Florida. Some of the items she suggests included in a humor cart are books, comics, and magazines; a surprise box with such items as funny glasses, animal noses, masks, puppets, gags, and card games; a collection of cartoons; and portable tape recorders and humorous cassettes (Gibson, 1995). If the budget allows, a videocassette recorder (VCR) in a locking portable cabinet and videotapes can add hours of enjoyment for patients. Some televisions come in combination with VCRs or digital video disc (DVD) players.

Wooten (1995) mentions that carts can be different shapes and sizes. Some places use carts that look like old library carts. Others use big red toolboxes on wheels that are full of drawers and cabinets that can be locked. If a big red toolbox on wheels is used, Wooten (1995) suggests decorating it so that it does not look like a crash cart.

Patti Bihn, RN, received a grant from the *Journal of Nursing Jocularity* to create a humor cart for the intensive care unit (ICU) at St. Joseph Mercy Hospital in Ann Arbor, Michigan. In sharing her struggle to start a humor cart, Bihn (1995) offers ideas that can help others find carts and gather equipment. Bihn searched for something inexpensive to use as a cart. She tried to get one donated but could not. She finally got a cart with six baskets in a rolling metal frame. After she obtained the cart, the next step was to fill it. Bihn (1995) shares what she included in her cart (Table 10-1).

Terry Bennett, an oncology nurse, helped start a humor cart at the Fox Chase Cancer Center in Philadelphia (Wooten, 1995). She found the nursing administration supportive of the effort, but the hos-

TABLE 10-1: EXAMPLES OF CONTENTS INCLUDED IN A HUMOR CART

- modeling compound
- rolls of smiley heart stickers
- crossword puzzle books
- videos and audiocassettes
- fake poop in a specimen container (some of the props are to share with staff as well as with patients)
- playing cards
- slide puzzles
- slinky
- pinwheel head boppers (these are "pinwheels attached to a headband and make an interesting sight when transferring a patient out of the unit") [p. 33]
- plastic duckies
- silly apparel, such as, witch hats, jester clothing, and goofy hats
- gold cardboard crowns and tinsel (which can be used for a patient's birthday or some other special event)
- rubber chicken (no cart is complete without such an item)
- giant clown scissors and glasses
- bubbles
- back scratchers.

(Bihn, 1995)

pital administration was not as enthusiastic. To convince them of the usefulness of the project, articles and news clippings about the benefits of humor and health were presented. With permission granted, she gathered her materials from many of the local retailers in the community. She wrote letters requesting donations and received many positive responses.

In an interview with Wooten (1995), Bennett shared that the most popular item among cancer patients was a video by Joe Kogel called *Life and*

Depth. Kogel is a cancer survivor who gives a funny presentation about using humor to maintain a positive attitude and keep up hopes. Bennett also found that some contemporary videos were enjoyed. *Wayne's World* was a preferred video among adolescents, and seniors preferred such actors as Charlie Chaplin, Buster Keaton, and Lucille Ball. She also noted that having some audiotapes and videotapes of peaceful environments, such as meadowlands or seashores, were appreciated.

Laugh Mobile

Research has spurred the use of humor programs in hospital settings. One such program is the "Laugh Mobile," developed by Ruth Hamilton, the founder of the Carolina Health and Humor Association (Carolina Ha Ha). The "Laugh Mobile" is part of the Duke University Medical Center Humor Project, a joint venture between Carolina Ha Ha and Duke Oncology Recreational Therapy, that was started in 1987 (Hamilton, 2003). The "Laugh Mobile" is a humor cart that takes materials to inpatient and outpatient cancer patients. Since its initial development, a new "Laugh Mobile" has been developed and is being marketed to medical facilities nationwide.

Humor Baskets

Humor baskets have smaller numbers of items than humor carts and humor rooms. They are commonly used by family caregivers to bring humor into the lives of loved ones who are at home. Wooten (1996) writes about one nurse, Cathy Johnson of Dartmouth-Hitchcock Medical Center in Lyme, New Hampshire, who felt a need to improve the mood of patients enduring lengthy hospitalizations and prolonged bed rest. Not having much financial backing, she found a large wicker basket that she filled with assorted toys and gadgets.

A fun addition to a humor basket is medicine bottles filled with humorous comments. Wooten (1996) suggests that it is a good idea to place jokes for different age-groups and genders into different jars and label them. This way, jokes that would more likely be of interest for a certain group can be easily found. Finding one-liners to place in the bottles can be fun and offers a lighthearted touch to the seriousness of illness. Some suggestions for one-liners are:

☺ I intend to live forever—so far, so good.

☺ When everything is coming your way, you're in the wrong lane.

☺ When I'm in my right mind, my left mind gets pretty crowded.

☺ Energizer Bunny arrested; charged with battery.

☺ Shin: a device for finding furniture in the dark.

☺ Laughing stock: cattle with a sense of humor.

☺ One of the great blessings about living in a democracy is that we have complete control over how we pay our taxes . . . cash, check, or money order.

Caring Clowns

No one expects a clown to be profound. No one expects a clown to be anything but funny. Look again! The clown will catch you off guard and speak directly to your heart—make you laugh at yourself and weep with the world.

Shobi Dobi, CLL

Caring clowns are clowns who work in various areas of health care, such as hospitals, long-term care facilities, and home care. They are usually people who are specially trained to be sensitive to the needs of sick people. Patty Wooten is a well-known clown who is also an RN. She states that caring clowns should be "sensitive, be able to read nonverbal body language, and possess good listening skills" (Wooten, 1992, p. 46).

In an article on clowning Dr. Patch Adams (2002) states, "Clowning needs to be context, not a therapy . . . Of course it is therapeutic" (¶ 9). Clowning is Adams' (2002) way of bringing love and joy to patients.

People commonly think of clowns being used in pediatrics, and indeed they are, but they can be a beneficial diversion for people of all ages. At one of the annual American Association for Therapeutic Humor (AATH) conferences, a person who acts as a mime in nursing homes had a running video of her experience working in a long-term care facility. One clip showed her working with a woman with dementia. The woman looked confused and disoriented at first. The mime sat down next to her and slowly drew her out. Toward the end of the clip, she was kidding along with the mime and smiling.

In 2001, a mortuary in the Phoenix area employed Eloise Cole as a bereavement specialist. What makes her unique is that she is a clown who uses her clown character, Rainbow, to help clients deal with fears, questions, guilt, and other emotions that are part of the grieving process. Cole (2001) shared her development of Rainbow with the audience at the 2001 AATH conference.

Rainbow was developed when Cole realized that she was heard in a different way when she used humor to talk about serious topics. She found that people tended to let down their defenses and hear what she was saying when humor was part of the process. Through her exploration of the use of humor, she became interested in the art of clowning. Rainbow offers a way for people to get in touch with their grief experience on an emotional level. Cole (2001) explains the process of Rainbow's development and work this way:

> I chose the name of Rainbow for the symbolism. I put together a 12-minute presentation that encapsulates some of the major dynamics of the mourning experience. Rainbow appears as a happy clown and then tells her audience a story from a time in her life when she was really down because, someone she loved had died.

> Using a variety of props, Rainbow talks about the pain of someone dying, the efforts to be strong and keep busy, and feeling

crazy. She uses props such as a feather duster for keeping busy, a world globe symbolizes carrying the weight of the world on her shoulders, and a crab puppet symbolizes feeling crabby and out of sorts. Rainbow moves through some of the elements of mourning and then realizes that she needs help. Again props are used to point out the need for rest and nutrition and the avoidance of alcohol and drugs. Rainbow then asks for help and for people to listen to her and her pain. She discovers that she can learn to change, grow, and find new rainbows.

One of the best-known caring clown projects is the Big Apple Circus Clown Care Unit which started in New York City (Wooten, 1996). The project is made up of professional clowns who visit pediatric patients. The program started in 1986 in New York after the death of the cofounder's brother. It has expanded to include at least 17 hospitals across the country (Yale-New Haven Children's Hospital, 2002). In 1996, the Hinda and Richard Rosenthal Center for Complementary and Alternative Medicine at Columbia University in New York presented a $150,000 grant for the study of the impact of clown therapy on children's well-being. The purpose of the grant was to investigate the effect clown visits have on decreasing physiological and psychological distress in children and adolescents during clinical procedures.

Three different reports are posted on the Rosenthal Center Web site concerning the results of the Clown Care Unit studies. Two of the studies discussed were pilot studies (Gorfinkle, Slater, Bagiella, Tager, & Labinsky, n.d.). One study looked at the effect of clowns on children undergoing venipunctures, infusaport access, intramuscular injection, or lumbar puncture. The children were ages 3 to 18 and were randomly assigned to clown visits at either visit 1 or visit 2. The results of this study showed no significant difference in observed child distress with the clown present. The doctors and nurses, however, found the procedures easier to perform when the clowns were present.

In the second study, 28 heart transplant recipients ages 6 to 20 were observed during two consecutive biopsies in a cardiac catheterization laboratory. During their second visit, participants were assigned to a clown or no-clown situation. Children who were exposed to the clowns showed a marginally significant decrease in observed child distress and a significant decrease in child self-reported distress. There was also a significant decrease in parent-rated child distress. However, these results failed to reach significance when baseline differences were covaried. In addition, doctors found the procedure more difficult to perform with the clowns present (Gorfinkle et al., n.d.).

The results of the third study indicate a significant decrease in observed child distress, child-reported distress, and parent-rated child distress when clowns were present during cardiac catheterization. Positive changes were seen in hospital caregivers behavior and mood when the clowns were around. The clowns were introduced to three new hospitals for this study, and all of them remained at the conclusion of the study (Richard and Hinda Rosenthal Center for Complementary and Alternative Medicine, 2003).

Developing a Caring Clown

Wooten (1996) found her inner clown in 1973 and started developing her clown characters soon after. Learning to be a clown is an educational process, and schools are devoted to that purpose. Wooten started her clown training with a Ringling Brothers Clown College graduate who was teaching a "clownology" course through San Diego State University. She started out with Scruffy the Clown and later developed Nancy Nurse. Nancy Nurse is a wild, redheaded clown who comes decked out with a combat belt filled with weapons, such as a bedpan, a urinal, an enema bucket, and over-sized syringes. She wears a stethoscope made from a garden hose with a toilet plunger, which she says "is great to use

on those big-hearted patients . . . it can also be used to relieve constipation" (Wooten, 1996, p. 144). She is bold and outspoken and controls both doctors and nurses. Her character is funny and nurses love her outrageous behavior and solutions to common problems. When asked to visit patients, however, Wooten learned that Nurse Nancy could be a little too bold and too boisterous for patients and their families. So guideline number one, make sure the character fits the purpose of the job.

In 1994, Nurse Kindheart, a sweet, white-haired nurse with a proper British accent was born. Nurse Kindheart demonstrates patience and kindness as she visits those in need of ministering. Being aware of the needs and reactions of patients and their families caused Wooten to develop this antithesis to Nancy Nurse. The contrast of the two clowns is distinct, with Nurse Nancy bringing tears of laughter, and Nurse Kindheart causing a feeling of comfortable amusement. The development of the right clown, like the development of a person as they travel through life, depends on the circumstances, the personality of the performer, and the sensitivity of the person from whom the clown develops.

Wooten (1996) suggests guidelines for clown visitations in Table 10-2.

So You Want to Be a Clown

Are you already a clown or would you like to take lessons to become more knowledgeable about clowning? If this area of caring interests you, attend training. There are a number of clown schools throughout the United States. *The Hospital Clown Newsletter* offers suggestions, shares ideas, and gives general support. Letting out the clown in you allows you to put more joy into your life and into the lives of others. Patty Wooten, in her book *Compassionate Laughter: Jest for Your Health,* has two chapters on clowning. One chapter offers ideas for different ways to present yourself.

The story in Table 10-3, from *The Hospital Clown Newsletter* at http://www.hospitalclown.com,

TABLE 10-2: GUIDELINES FOR CLOWN VISITATIONS

☺ Visits should be pre-approved and scheduled.

☺ Visits should occur between 9 a.m. and 8 p.m.

☺ Clowns should check in at the nursing station and obtain feedback about and suggestions for patient visits.

☺ Clowns should request the staff to accompany them to the patient's room on the first visit.

☺ Prior to entering the room, clowns should request permission from the patient to visit.

☺ Clowns should not move patients or manipulate hospital equipment. The staff should be called if necessary.

☺ Gifts should be approved by the staff before being given to patients.

☺ Visits should be limited to 10 minutes, unless staff permits longer visits.

☺ Clowns should stop at the nursing station after visits are completed to obtain any other requests or notify the staff that they are leaving.

(Wooten, 1996)

portrays the essence of what a hospital clown does. The clown stays in character, reaches out with his or her heart, brings joy and comfort to those around him or her, and then finds a way to let go of the sorrows and burdens of others.

Dr. Patch Adams (2002) believes all members of a hospital staff should think about being clowns. He feels that thinking about clowning (or humor, love, and joy) as therapy and the clown as a specialist who does the clowning might lead others to think they do not have to help bring love, humor, or joy to the patient. He states, "I want to put in an encouragement for each person, professional clown or not, to imagine that what they do each day can be a potent part of creating a context of love and fun" (Adams, 2002, ¶ 17). He contends that, if each of us brought joy and comfort to those around us, our jobs would be more rewarding and those around us would experience less suffering.

Bringing Clowns into a Facility

With all of the literature available on the importance of humor and with the development of caring clown programs, one would think that health care facility administrations would be thrilled to have someone offer to start such a program. This is often not the case. Shobhana Schwebke (n.d.), who goes by the clown name Shobie Dobie and is the editor

of *The Hospital Clown Newsletter,* feels that part of the problem is an administration's need to put clowns in hospital categories. She states, "Hospital care is a scientific-based discipline; the clown is a heart-based discipline" (¶3). Approaching an administration can be a challenge. Wooten (1996) offers the following suggestions:

- The first visit to a hospital or nursing home should be done wearing street clothes.

- Meet with appropriate staff (for example, the child development specialist or nursing supervisor).

- Obtain permission and establish guidelines. (Be sure to bring suggestions with you because many facilities do not have guidelines for entertainers who visit patients.)

- Present a professional manner.

- Convince the administration of your intent to work with the system to develop a program that will benefit the facility and the patients.

THE PLANNING STAGES

Humor rooms, humor carts, comedy via closed-circuit television, and hospital clowns are all examples of how to bring therapeutic humor into a facility. Whatever type of program a facility wants

TABLE 10-3: I LOVE YOU WOLLIE

(as told to Shobi by Jackie Garner)

I was packing to go to a convention when I got a call from a hospital I'd never been to. I don't know how they found out about Lolli. They said "We have a little boy in ICU. Could you come as fast as you can?" I had already packed my costume, but when I heard ICU, I had Lolli clowned up and at that hospital in 30 minutes. I had never and never since put on my makeup that fast. I could never makeup again that fast or that well except that it was something that I was called to do.

I get up to Pediatric ICU and as soon as the elevator doors open you can hear crying and moaning cause these kids don't like being there and they're hurting. Now ICU is normally glassed rooms, because they have to be able to see everything. You can see all the children in their beds. You haven't been called to see them, but all those children are watching you. So I go into a little boy's room – his name was Vincent. He is four and a half years old. And again you could hear moaning. I come around the corner and in character voice say "Hello." The doctor says, "You must be Lolli!" "Yes, and who is this handsome boy?" The doctor introduces "This is Vincent." Lolli continues "Are you married? Are you engaged to anyone?" He doesn't say anything, he is just looking at me, but his eyes are smiling. He's not scared of me after all he's four and one-half.

The doctor says, "Lolli, do you mind if we bring in a rocking chair? Would you like to sit in a rocking chair and hold Vincent?" Lolli answered "Sure would." So, they brought in this beautiful white rocking chair. And again I can be seen by all the other children all around me from their beds. They lay a pad across my lap and they lay Vincent in my arms, and he is so close. His eyes immediately go to my jeweled heart nose. He's checking out my hair, my face and all the bright colors. And Mama is looking right over my left shoulder and Daddy's looking right over my right shoulder, so we are all close. "Lolli loves you, Vincent."

I can tell he wants to touch my nose. So I take his finger and push my nose and laugh. "This is little Lolli's laugh button. Tee hee, Little Lolli loves you, Vincent." Mama's over the left shoulder saying "I love you, baby" and Daddy says "It's O.K. son, Daddy's here."

About 30 minutes goes by – just quiet time of giggles and nose pushing. In that time I knew this child like my own. We made a connection that no one could ever separate. Yet, he had not said one word to me. All of a sudden, Vincent pushes my nose again and he giggles all the way to his toes. Just giggles. Not one tear. There was no pain. This is what happens, something magical happens when a clown is there with a child in a one-on-one.

He just had the sweetest smile in his eyes and face. And each time I would say "Little Lolli loves you, Vincent," and Mama and Daddy would say "I'm here, I love you." This time I pushed my nose and giggled and said, "I love you." He took a breath and spoke, "I love you, Wollie." I wanted to change my name to Wollie, right there. Then he said "I love you, Mommy. I love you, Daddy." And with this, his eyes went up to my eyes and my nose. "You want to push my nose again." So I took his little finger and pushed my nose. As I said "Little Lolli loves you, Vincent," he takes in the deepest breath, his smile broadens and his eyes are glistening. Then he breathes out his last breath. He dies in Lolli's arms.

The doctor comes over and takes Vincent from my arms and the mother and father go with him and I'm thinking, I've got to get out of here. I've got to run. But I look up at all those kids around me. They don't know what just happened. They are watching my every move. I am the clown. I am not Jackie Garner dressed as Lollibelle - I am Lolli to them. I am the only clown they may ever see. So I wave "Hello" in Lolli's character voice, but I'm thinking I've got to get out of here. I go out the door and there is a child right there. "Hello, Lolli loves you." I'm thinking, if I can just get to the elevator, I can let this out. I'm half way down the hall and I can see the elevator button. "Hello, Hi" waving to the other children. Inside me, the mother I am, is screaming, but these kids don't see this. It does not show on my face, because I am Little Lolli the clown.

Jackie Garner cannot do this. God has a part in this, something greater has control of this for you when you do this with all your heart and you want to help the kids. He's going to help you do it. That's the only way you are going to get through it. I'm not a great person. I'm not superwoman. I just have to let go and let Him help me handle it.

So, I'm almost to the elevator, and here come Vincent's Dad. "Clown, wait!" Tears are running down his face and he is reaching into his pocket. "What do I owe you?" I answer softly "Nothing, what do I owe you?" And I leaned over and whispered into his ear. "There are children watching and I have to stay in clown character." And as I go to the elevator I wave. "I love you, Daddy. Bye! Bye!" I push the button and I see the down light flashing, but here comes the mother crying. "Lolli, please I need to see you." I answer in character "Okay, Mom." And I think that was the longest walk I ever made in my life – back down the hall toward the mother. When I get there, Mom just falls into my arms – and she is sobbing into my costume – and I can feel her tears go past my hair and down my neck. "Lolli, he never got to go to Disney World, my baby never even got to see the circus and all of that. Oh, did you notice the way he went, there was no pain. He was smiling, he was giggling." And Lolli whispered in her ear, "I know, Mom. He's going to be fine. You're going to see him someday and you're going to take up just were you left off. But other children are watching Lolli. I love you and from one mommy to another I do understand. Thank you for letting me be a part of this." She looked up, "We will never forget you, Lolli." Daddy comes out and they walk back down the hall. And there I am trying to get back to the elevator, again, in character waving to the children "Hello, Hi, Little Lolli loves you." The children for all they knew, the child fell asleep in my arms.

The elevator door opens and sure enough there was a mom inside with two kids. "Hello!" I'm thinking, soon I'll be outside and I can let go. And the lobby was full of kids, and the parking lot looked like Disney World. "Hello! How ya doing?" I get on the freeway and everyone is driving by waving at the clown – "Oh look there is a clown. Hello, Clown." I'm thinking, God find me a dirt road please! And I found one right after I asked for it. I drove down that road and there wasn't a soul on the road and I was able to let go and cry. These to me are the true tears of a clown. When you are touched by something and you realize that you are being used to touch and offer healing. Be it death or whatever, you never know what you are going to be asked to do.

Reprinted with permission from *The Hospital Clown Newsletter* Web site at http://www.hospitalclown.com/InfoPages/storiesTable.htm

to implement, it takes time and money to put it all together. Convincing the administration of the importance of adding humor to the hospital environment may also take time and effort. After all, hospitals are about serious business. Using research to support your argument can help convince the administration that humor can be an inexpensive tool to increase patient health and satisfaction with the care they receive.

When planning a project, keep in mind the audience for the humor. If the audience is very young children or older adults, videos and cassette tapes may need to be shorter to accommodate shorter attention spans. Cultural issues are also an important consideration. Are most of the patients in the facility Mexican, Cuban, or African American? Can you get material that would be of interest to that cultural group? These are just some questions to consider.

Getting Started

It is a good idea to form a committee of people who are interested in providing some type of humor program in your facility. It is suggested to include someone from pastoral care, a volunteer from the volunteer program, someone from the nursing department, someone from physical therapy or occupational therapy, a social service person, and someone from administration (Gibson, 1995).

Once the committee has been organized, it is time to think about what the committee would like to see developed with the resources that might be available. Having knowledge of what other facilities have done to bring humor to their patients or residents (in the case of long-term care facilities) can help identify possibilities. Gibson (1995) cautions that the committee should go slow and not try to serve everybody in the beginning. She recommends starting on one unit and getting the staff and patients motivated on that unit.

Cost Concerns

To help determine how much the project will cost, it is necessary to brainstorm. A good starting place would be to think about:

- where or what will be used, such as the waiting room, humor baskets, or humor carts
- how to designate the area
- what type of program the facility can afford
- where financing might be available
- how the facility will advertise the program
- where materials might come from.

Think about what materials the program will have to pay for and what materials might be available from staff, patients, and the community. The most popular items for comedy carts, humor rooms, and baskets are humorous video or audio tapes, cartoon albums, humorous books, gag items, and props such as Groucho glasses or clowns' noses.

Finding funding might require some creativity. Gibson (1995) recommends contacting the local Rotary, Kiwanis, and Women's Leagues to ask them to sponsor a program at your facility. Contact local merchants to see if they would be willing to donate equipment, videos, or books. Contact the volunteer committee of the hospital and see if volunteers would be willing to have a fundraiser to raise money for the project. One hospital in Pennsylvania put an advertisement in the local newspaper asking for humorous items (Gibson, 1995). They ended up receiving thousands of items.

Some hospitals have applied to the Humor Project, a program in Saratoga Springs, New York, founded and directed by Joel Goodman, for humor research grants to start programs. In 1996, Intergris Baptist Hospital Medical Center in Oklahoma City started a Medical Institute for Recovery Through Humor (MIRTH) program in its 20-bed skilled nursing facility (Foltz-Gray, 1998). Goodman went to the facility to do an hour-long training session. The Humor Project offered MIRTH a $3,000 grant to start the project, which serves as a research vehicle, a humor resource center, and a place of support for patients, family, and staff.

Advertising

In order for a project to work, people need to know about it. Having a name for the project is helpful. Communication about the project is important. Suggested means of advertising the project include calling the press, putting information about the project in the hospital newsletter, and having a party to celebrate the opening of the project (Gibson, 1995). Talk about the project in staff meetings, and make sure that the physicians know about it. Get creative. The more people who know about the project, the more likely it is to be successful.

Supplies

Storing supplies can be a challenge. Hospitals are always looking for new places to store things. In the beginning, a cart that can be locked might be the best idea, unless a room is available. The cart can be placed somewhere visible, decorated with bright colors, and labeled so people know what it is. This tactic serves as another form of advertising as well as a place to store the humor equipment.

The program must have a method to account for and monitor the supplies. Gibson (1995) learned that people did not always return items that were used, and supplies disappeared. Designing a sign-out sheet is a good precautionary measure. The sheet can include the name of the person who uses the material, the department or room number, the resource taken (such as game, magazine, or videotape), and a place to sign it back into the supply area.

Having an inventory of the supplies is important. Gibson (1995) suggests putting numbers on books, videos, and cassette tapes so that they can be cataloged. Doing so also helps keep a record of what you have. Cataloging also makes it easier for patients to know what is available. Utilize volunteers to help with this duty.

Supplies may be obtained through a number of sources. Bihn (1995) shares her experience of gathering supplies for a humor cart for the intensive care unit (ICU) at St. Joseph Mercy Hospital in Ann Arbor, Michigan. Some of the supplies were ordered from various companies, but she was also able to obtain donations from a local video store and a novelty store. The video store donated three comedies, and the novelty store donated a rubber chicken, jumbo sunglasses, and jumbo scissors.

Training

Training the volunteers and staff who will work with the humor program and providing inservice programs on the humor project are important. The volunteers who will work with the program need to be oriented to hospital policies and to the lay out of the facility.

In addition, the people who are working with the program need to know their roles (Gibson, 1995). Guidelines regarding expectations need to be developed and included in the training sessions. As volunteers start to work, keep them busy so they do not get bored, especially in the beginning of the program (Gibson, 1995). Encourage them to sit with or play checkers with patients to promote involvement.

Volunteers need to know that not everyone will be interested or feel well enough to participate in humor activities. They also need to know that they should not touch patients or be loud, especially if they are acting as clowns. Discourage volunteers from asking, "How are you today?" because "we want to divert [patients] from the 'poor me' angle" (Gibson, 1995, p. 122). Instead, encourage them to ask, "What can I offer you today?" Those involved in the humor project must understand that humor should not be forced on anybody.

HUMORING THE STAFF

The previously mentioned interventions discuss ways to bring humor to patients, but what about the staff? Hospital staff is under a lot of stress on a daily basis. Nursing staff members are often overworked and work in difficult situations. The present nursing shortage adds to the normal stress of caring for people who are seriously ill or may be dying, fearful, or in pain. Adding humor to a staff's daily working environment can help increase morale, improve relations between different departments, and help decrease the stress level.

Some hospitals have used humor during the celebration of nurses' week. A small hospital in southwestern Arizona contacted three nurses who call themselves the Ha Ha Sisterhood to come in and do something on humor and health for the nursing staff. These three nurses started out presenting the program for the local community college. One nurse is an emergency room supervisor, and the other two nurses are educators at the local community college. They come together periodically to educate and share the joy of humor. The program offers nurses a chance to laugh, let their hair down, and let go of the stresses of the day. For example, before one program started, a member of the dietary staff borrowed one of the wigs and had a fun time laughing and sharing with her coworkers.

Nurses have also been known to take items off of their facility's humor cart to use with fellow staff members to lighten the daily load. Another way to introduce humor into the work environment is to place a bulletin board at the nurses' station with space for sharing cartoons, puns, and jokes. One effective way for healthcare providers to find stress release is to generate and share in humorous situations. Doing so does not make the nurse unprofessional, as some may think; rather, it increases creativity and boosts morale.

SUMMARY

There are a number of ways to provide humor intervention in medical facilities. Humor rooms, humor carts, and humor baskets are three common examples. Caring clowns are specially trained people who can bring laughter and play to those who are ill. Whatever humor intervention is used, it takes time and energy to develop a program, but patients benefit from the experience in immeasurable ways.

EXAM QUESTIONS

CHAPTER 10
Questions 82-90

82. The difference between a humor cart and a humor room is

    a. humor carts have videos in them and humor rooms do not.

    b. humor rooms are easier to supply than humor carts.

    c. humor rooms have props, such as clown noses, and humor carts do not.

    d. humor carts are mobile and provide greater patient access.

83. According to oncology nurse Terry Bennett, a good video to have in a humor cart is

    a. *Shrek.*

    b. *Rambo.*

    c. *Star Wars.*

    d. *Life and Depth.*

84. Caring clowns are

    a. circus clowns who make hospital visits.

    b. clowns who work in all areas of healthcare.

    c. always professional actors.

    d. clowns who work only with children.

85. Eloise Cole (Rainbow) uses her clown character to help people who are

    a. bereaved.

    b. mentally ill.

    c. children.

    d. elderly.

86. The *best* way to become a Caring Clown is to

    a. attend training at a clown school.

    b. just have the desire to be funny.

    c. go with your natural instincts.

    d. be sure you have a gimmick.

87. A recommended guideline for Caring Clowns to follow during visitations is

    a. stay in the room as long as the patient wants.

    b. always give the patient something to remember you by.

    c. ask the patient for permission to enter the room.

    d. every visit should be made with a nurse present in the room.

88. When considering starting a humor program in a facility, the *most* appropriate way of helping administration *understand the benefits* of a humor program would be to

    a. present research information about the benefits of humor.

    b. have a clown come to the facility in costume to 'clown' with the administration.

    c. form a committee to persuade the administration to start a program.

    d. immediately start a program to prove how successful it can be.

89. A characteristic of humor projects is that they

    a. are spontaneous and unplanned.

    b. usually involve only one person.

    c. take thought and planning.

    d. do not require time and money.

90. When training volunteers to work in a humor program, it is essential that they know

    a. everyone is going to be happy to see them.

    b. they can touch the patient.

    c. not everyone will be interested or well enough to see them.

    d. their presence is important to all patients.

CHAPTER 11

HUMOR RX FOR YOUR PRACTICE

CHAPTER OBJECTIVES

After completing this chapter, the reader will be able to discuss ways to engage in humorous interchanges with patients, colleagues, and other healthcare providers.

LEARNING OBJECTIVES

After studying this chapter, the reader will be able to

1. discuss ways to bring humor into his or her own life.

2. identify appropriate humor.

3. recognize when it is inappropriate to use humor with a patient.

4. discuss ways to add more humor into the work environment.

INTRODUCTION

This chapter looks at interventions that can add humor into your nursing practice. It discusses ways to increase humor during patient care as well as ways to use humor with colleagues and other healthcare team members. Suggestions for improving or increasing personal humor experiences are also shared.

FOR YOURSELF

To bring humor into the healthcare environment, a sense of playfulness is helpful. As noted in the theory section of this course, playfulness is an essential component of humor. It helps us lighten up. It does what Joel Goodman of the Humor Project tells his audience to do: It lets you put the "elf" in "yourself." Until you find the humor within you, it can be hard to share humor with others. The following list suggests ways to add more humor into your life including some real-life examples:

☺ Watch funny movies.

☺ Watch sitcoms or comedy channels.

☺ Find the funny things in everyday situations.

— A woman with dementia was cold, so she turned up the thermostat. Her husband became upset that she did this, so he turned the thermostat down and the air conditioner came on. It eventually became very cold in the house. The woman's daughter-in-law was using the telephone; her son and husband were watching television. Suddenly, the woman, who used to be very prim and proper, came out of the bedroom dressed in her underwear and trying to put on her robe. The only problem was that she was trying to put her foot into the sleeve of the robe. Although this was really sad to see, the daughter-in-law could not help smiling at the ridiculous site and the apparent oblivion of the woman's husband and son—neither of whom got up to help until the daughter-in-law stopped her conversation on the phone long enough to say, "Someone please help Mom."

— A student is at a library checking out some books. The student hands her card to the library assistant. The assistant looks at the card and says, "Oh, you've expired." The student looks around, looks back at the assistant, and says, "I don't think so."

— You are sitting in a gynecologist's office filling out a form. You get to a question that reads, "Are you presently sexually active." Mind you, you are sitting in the doctor's waiting room. You think that there should be a box for "not right at this moment."

☺ Think about and share an embarrassing story.

— A lady went into a store dressing room to try on some bathing suits. As she went to put her leg into the leg of one suit, she lost her balance and fell out of the dressing room, in clear view of everyone standing outside the room.

— A woman was walking down a busy city street with her husband and a male friend. Suddenly a car stopped and a woman said to the lady, "Excuse me honey, but your skirt is caught in your pantyhose." And neither one of the men had noticed.

— Many years ago, a candy striper who was very short was preparing to throw laundry down the laundry shoot. The laundry cart was very tall. As she reached in to get the laundry, she fell into the laundry basket. There she was with her feet in the air and her head in the cart. The head nurse walked by and said, "Okay, Nancy, get yourself out of there." Eventually, they had to obtain help to get her out.

☺ Keep a humor log or journal of jokes, experiences, puns, cartoons, and stories that made you laugh each day.

— A woman who had a bad skin condition kept a humor diary as a way of improving her sense of humor. The more humor she found, the more she began to enjoy things around her, and the better her skin condition became.

☺ Blow bubbles

— Pens that have bubbles on one end make great items to carry with you. One day, a 3-year-old was crying and acting up in the airport. Out came the bubbles. For 15 minutes, the child stopped crying and the grown-ups smiled. The atmosphere became less tense.

☺ Collect stress-releasing toys. Examples of great toys are clown noses, Groucho glasses, and toys that make animal noises or growl.

— Clown noses work great in traffic. One "jollyologist" likes to put on a red clown nose and watch all the people around him when they notice it.

— One lady with cancer received a toy that looked like a funny face. When she squeezed it, the eyes and tongue popped out. Whenever she was feeling stressed, she would pull out the face and squeeze.

— A counseling student was doing her internship at a community college. One of the counselors had just lost her husband and was having a number of difficult days. Plus, it was the beginning of registration and the tension level was high. One day, the student brought in a stuffed dinosaur that growled when it was squeezed. The toy was such a big hit with the counselor that she bought the counselor a baby dinosaur that did not have as loud of a roar. One day, the student heard the growl of the baby dinosaur many times. Thinking the counselor was having a bad day, she stopped in to say hello and found a member of the office staff there instead. The office worker explained that she was going through a really difficult time and the growl of the baby dinosaur brought a smile to her face.

— Collect toys when you see them. For example, a few years ago, a discount store was selling a little box that looked like a shipping box. At one corner, it looked as if an eye was peeking out. If you pushed the button on the other corner, the box would shake and a little voice could be heard: "Help! Help! Somebody let me out of here."

☺ Watch children at play.

☺ Play with children.

☺ Watch the antics of animals.

☺ Take silly photos of yourself.

— Go to a photo booth or use a Polaroid camera and take pictures of yourself making funny faces or doing something silly. Keep the photo where you will look at it to remind yourself to maintain a playful attitude.

☺ Make a list of things that you have fun doing and do two of them each day.

☺ Place reminders to take time for play in key areas (such as on a bathroom mirror, refrigerator, or desk).

☺ Hang around people who have positive attitudes and make you laugh. When you are around negative people, they bring you down. Find people who find enjoyment in life and can laugh at the everyday annoyances. When you are with others who are playful and help you laugh, you add that much more humor to your life.

☺ Make up a humor "first-aid kit" containing items that make you laugh. The kit might contain such items as funny cartoons, cards, bumper stickers, bouncing balls, whistles, or

funny hats. When you or someone you know is down, pull out something from the kit.

☺ Make a list of five things that make you smile. Then try to find five new things every day.

☺ Use exaggeration. Take a bad day at work and really blow it out of proportion. The more exaggeration, the better. Eventually, the humor in the situation is likely to come out. Share it with co-workers and have them add to the exaggeration.

☺ Smile, even if you do not feel like it. Your face does not know the difference between the real thing and a forced smile, and it can help lighten your mood. Also, others will wonder what you are up to!

☺ Do something you do not normally do. Doing or saying something unexpected causes you and others to pause and usually results in a smile or even a laugh.

— Rather than answer "I'm fine" when someone asks how you are, say something like, "It depends on who you ask, but I think I'm great!"

— One humor presenter shared how, occasionally, at a toll booth he would pay for the car behind him, and then watch the surprised and quizzical expressions on the faces of the people in the car as they tried to figure out what happened and why.

☺ Declare a funny hat day at work. (Obtain administration's permission first.) It is fun for the staff as well as for the patients.

☺ Wear or carry something humorous.

— A lady at a local bagel shop wears a different headpiece every day. She has a headband with springs to which she attaches items. Some days it has windmills on it, other days it has hearts that wiggle or multicolored balls.

— Find a pen that is different, such as one that looks like a syringe or one that holds bubble soap and a wand.

☺ Laugh at life's daily slip-ups.

— When you put the cereal in the refrigerator or the milk in the cabinet, laugh about it.

☺ Laugh it up. A hearty belly laugh may be better for you than a demure giggle.

HUMOR AND PATIENT CARE

We know that using humor with patients is a way of establishing rapport, communicating in a nonthreatening manner, enhancing teaching opportunities, and decreasing stress and anxiety. Humor may be initiated by the patient or the nurse. In some situations, such as crises, the nurse commonly waits for the patient to be the initiator. If the nurse chooses to be the initiator, it is best to follow the advice of Karyn Buxman (1996): Be sure you follow the "Five Rights of Humor Administration" (Table 11-1).

TABLE 11-1: THE FIVE RIGHTS OF HUMOR ADMINISTRATION
☺ Right patient
☺ Right type
☺ Right time
☺ Right amount
☺ Right route.
(Buxman, 1996)

The type of humor that is most often a part of the interaction between patient and nurse is situational humor. It occurs spontaneously and reflects the present situation between nurse and patient. This type of humor can offer a sense of control in a powerless situation. As Klein (n.d.) states, "Laughter is a powerful tool in a powerless situation" (¶ 5). It can offer hope and an upper hand to patients who are experiencing physical and mental loss. Allen Klein (n.d.) offers sound advice when it comes to using humor:

The safest way . . . is to first establish a rapport with the patient. Then look for humor by listening to what the patient jokes about. Above all, do not go into a patient's room with a battery of jokes. First, jokes can be offensive, and second, when you enter the room of someone who is ill, you have no knowledge whether they will be receptive to your kidding around. (¶6)

Paying attention to the words used to create the humor can give the nurse clues about the type of humor a patient is comfortable with. Humor can also cover up issues that may need to be explored. For this reason, nurses need to think of humor as a therapeutic clue from which to build. For example, a dying patient says to a nurse, "I wish we had pop-up buttons like turkeys, so we'd know when we were done!" (Robinson, 1991, p. 52). The message here has something to do with the anxiety of waiting to die. An alert nurse can use this statement to open up communication regarding the patient's concern.

Culture, personality, level of stress, pain, and depression are all factors that need to be considered when initiating or responding to humor with patients. Initiating humor with terminally ill patients requires sensitivity. Terminally ill participants of a study by Herth (1995) suggested that attempts at humor by health care providers should begin slowly using lighthearted responses, such as smiling, winking, or playful comments (Herth, 1995). "Openness to fun on the clinician's part can provide the opportunity for the seriously ill individual to open up to humor" (Herth, 1995, p. 224).

A gentleman in the hospital had asked his wife to bring in some of his toys. One of them was a "Y-2-K Bug" that made the sound of glass crashing when you hit the bottom. It was not uncommon for members of the staff to come in and borrow his toys to cause smiles and laughter in the life of other patients. Plus, the doctors would start their rounds by playing with his toys. It delighted him to be able to provide that type of entertainment for others, and the staff knew it. The toys also gave staff permission to joke with him. Supporting the use of toys is one of the ways nurses can help support and encourage humor use by patients.

Prior to initiating humor with a patient, it is helpful to know what that particular patient finds funny. A formal method of doing this would be to use the humor assessment offered in chapter 6. A full assessment may not always be needed. Ask one assessment question and build on it. For example: "What is your favorite sitcom?" When the patient answers, respond with, "What is it about the program that you like?" As the discussion progresses, ask the patient to share a favorite scene. As the patient shares, note if the patient's mood lightens. It probably will. After all, who can recall the Lucille Ball scene where she is stomping on the grapes and not begin to at least smile?

Above all else, smile whenever and wherever appropriate. The connection between nurse and patient, or nurse and visitor, grows from the smile. Stay alert to the patient's use of humor, and look for times when humor can be interjected. Just remember the Five Rights and remain alert for the right as well as the wrong time.

Personal Insight

During the development of my dissertation, I found that simply asking about participants' use of humor in coping with breast cancer increased their awareness of how they use humor in their lives. The result for a number of participants was to deliberately increase and be aware of humor in their lives. So, a simple question might be, "What role has humor had in your life?" Approaching the subject, giving the patient permission to think about and pursue humor, is a simple intervention that can help lead the patient to moments of coping humor.

Add humor to your patient education. Remember that humor catches the imagination, can

decrease tension, and may increase learning. Be alert to the patient's use of humor as a message of concern, and use that as a means of leading into teaching situations. Caring requires that nurses be alert for opportunities to teach patients the way to better health, be it for prevention or for managing a disease process. Smile; it helps the patient feel more at ease, and decreased tension leads to increased retention of information.

THE WRONG TIME, THE WRONG TYPE

There are times when humor is not appropriate. For humor to be effective, nurses must be alert for the right time to use it. At times, humor can be hurtful and even detrimental. As mentioned in chapter 7, the survivor of a disaster or crisis might initiate humor, but initiation by the nurse during the immediate crisis situation is often inappropriate .

In some cases, what the patient needs to do is cry or yell, or be quiet and alone. Watch for those times. Encourage patients to do what they need to do at that time. Sometimes just saying the right words at the right time is what a patient needs. Sometimes what a patient needs to hear is "this stinks" or "this sucks."

The wrong type of humor can cause discomfort or even anger. Avoid joking that pokes fun at other individuals or groups. Using put downs, ethnic jokes, "anti-" jokes (jokes that are negative toward men, women, or religious or ethnic groups) are usually hurtful. Sarcasm and gallows humor can also be hurtful.

HUMOR INTERVENTIONS FOR SURVIVING WORK-INDUCED STRESS

A very good bit of advice when work is stress-filled is to take your work seriously and yourself lightly. Burnout, or "compassion fatigue" as it has been called, is a hazard anyone in a helping profession faces. During times of burnout, humor can be hard to find. However, if we can manage to tap into our funny bone, laughter and play change thinking and attitudes and can do a lot to prevent or decrease the sense of apathy that burnout can cause.

There are many stressors within the healthcare environment. When staff members are stressed, overworked, and out of sorts, it is a good idea to bring some humor into the environment. Things that staff can do for themselves include sharing cartoons on bulletin boards, taking funny photos and sharing them, telling jokes, supporting and applauding efforts of staff members, giving each other a standing ovation, and wearing a humorous item to work.

This is the story of what one person did to lighten her mood and get her point across:

The head nurse had left her job and one of the staff nurses was assigned to be "schedule coordinator." Everyone on the floor did his or her own scheduling, but she was the overseer who checked for over- or understaffing, and made appropriate changes. She made enemies in the process. After a few months of hate mail, she posted the following message.

"Following the path of our Congressmen and Senators, I am pleased to inform you I will now be accepting bribes. Twenty dollars per request, regular weekday. Twenty-five dollars per holiday or weekend request. Guaranteed fulfillment of your request! The money will go to my Special Defense Fund. I've hired a bodyguard to protect me from the wrath of all of you!"

SUMMARY

Sometimes humor happens spontaneously and works as a means of connection between the nurse and patient or the nurse and another health-care provider. Either way, it is helpful for nurses to work at putting more humor into their lives so that they are more likely to use and respond to humor with patients. So, do something outrageous. Wear a button that has a smile on it or a catchy phrase. Put cartoons where staff can enjoy them. Smile; it will not only make you feel better, but it will have a positive effect on everyone around you.

There are times when humor is appropriate, and times when it is not. There are also certain types of humor that do not have a place in the healthcare setting. Stay away from sarcasm, unless it is aimed at yourself. Do not tell cultural or political jokes. Most of all, be sensitive to others and honor your ability to find funny things in everyday experiences.

EXAM QUESTIONS

CHAPTER 11
Questions 91-100

91. You are late for work. Traffic is backed up and barely moving because of an accident. Something needs to be done to break your tension and the tension of the drivers around you. Taking the advice of this text, you

    a. start screaming.

    b. close your eyes and hope the other drivers will wake you up.

    c. put on a clown nose.

    d. take out a magazine and start reading.

92. An easy way for a person to add a sense of happiness to life is to

    a. think about all the problems he or she has.

    b. just smile.

    c. buy joke books.

    d. party frequently.

93. The Five Rights of Humor Administration are

    a. right patient, right trigger, right time, right amount, right route.

    b. right patient, right type, right focus, right amount, right route.

    c. right patient, right type, right time, right amount, right cue.

    d. right patient, right type, right time, right amount, right route.

94. The most common type of humor between patient and nurse is

    a. situational.

    b. planned.

    c. programmed.

    d. joking.

95. A patient has been admitted with a diagnosis of congestive heart failure. The nurse is concerned about the patient's sad mood and decides that humor might be appropriate. Taking the advice of Alan Klein, she decides to

    a. go into the room with a few jokes she can share.

    b. wear a clown nose when entering the room.

    c. bring a book of *The Far Side* jokes with her into the room.

    d. establish rapport and listen for clues from the patient.

96. A nurse walks into a patient's room. The patient starts screaming that nobody has been in to see her in hours. The nurse knows the aide had been in the room 5 minutes earlier. The most appropriate response would be

    a. to find something humorous in this situation.

    b. to tell the patient to calm down and then do the task he or she entered the room to do.

    c. to tell the patient a joke about call lights.

    d. to let the patient vent and then ask an open-ended question to determine the underlying problem.

97. A new patient is being admitted for surgery. It is apparent that she is nervous. The most appropriate way to help relieve some of the tension would be to bring her a hospital gown and say,

    a. "Here, take off all your clothes and put this on."

    b. "I need to get your blood pressure, pulse, and temperature."

    c. "Please put on our Paris original."

    d. "The OR team will be here soon."

98. One way to help prevent compassion fatigue is to

    a. find ways to play.

    b. share your complaints with others.

    c. become politically active.

    d. put in more hours at work.

99. The type of humor that should be avoided by the nurse is

    a. work-related humor.

    b. puns.

    c. ethnic jokes.

    d. situational humor.

100. Tensions were rising on the medical unit. One of the nurses decided to add some humor to try and decrease the tension. He wanted to do something that all might be able to enjoy. The best way for him to do this is to

    a. share cartoons pertaining to healthcare mishaps.

    b. share ethnic jokes with the staff.

    c. play practical jokes on his coworkers.

    d. bring comedy videos for the staff to watch.

This concludes the final examination.

WEB RESOURCES

Allen Klein, The Jollyologist

Allen Klein is an award-winning professional speaker and best-selling author of such books as *The Healing Power of Humor, The Courage to Laugh,* and *Up Words for Down Days.* His Web site contains humor-related articles, links to other humor sites, and a listing of recommended humor books.

http://www.allenklein.com/

Art Gliner Center for Humor Studies

This center offers a scholarship for graduate student internship proposals to work on training that will lead to socially useful applications of humor. There is a link to essays on humor as well as other humor sites.

http://www.humorcenter.umd.edu

Good Humor, Good Health

This site has an article written by David S. Sobel, MD, MPH, and Robert Ornstein, PhD, that discusses how humor can be used to stay healthy.

http://www.kaiserpermanente.org/toyourhealth/hottopics/sobel/humor.html

How Laughter Works

This article, from the How Stuff Works Web site, looks at what happens in our brains when we laugh, what makes us laugh, and how laughter can make us healthier and happier. The article ends with tips for putting more laughter into our lives and links to other useful Web sites.

http://www.howstuffworks.com/laughter

Humor for Your Health

This Canadian organization was launched to empower people to obtain greater health and happiness through the understanding and application of their own unique sense of humor. The site has articles on the ancient history of humor and health, using humor at work and at school, the keys to telling jokes, surviving grief with humor, appropriate and inappropriate humor, and much more!

http://humorforyourhealth.com

Humor Matters

Presented by Dr. Steven Sultanoff, former President of the Association for Applied and Therapeutic Humor, this Web site is dedicated to educate, inform, and help visitors network and locate resources that focus on humor and its relation to health and healing.

http://humormatters.com

Humor Research

This page has great links to information about humor research, humor researchers web pages where many of the researchers offer information about the research they have done, and a list of courses being taught about humor.

http://www.uni-duesseldorf.de/WWW/MathNat/Ruch/humor.html

Jest for the Health of It!

Patty Wooten has put together this great Web site for information on humor; buying humor books, tapes, or other products; therapeutic clowning; and humor links.

http://www.jesthealth.com

Laughter Remedy

This web page was created by Paul McGhee. There is information about the health benefits of humor as well as how individuals, organizations and support groups can benefit from humor.

http://www.laughterremedy.com

Nursing & Medical Humor links on: The Nurse Friendly

This site offers humorous stories and nursing jokes as well as information on travel nursing, home businesses, and other general information.

http://www.nursinghumor.com

Rx Laughter

This site provides information on the study of laughter in children.

http://www.rxlaughter.org/

The Association for Applied and Therapeutic Humor

This is a great Web site that contains articles, general information, and information on conferences.

http://www.aath.org/

The Humor Collection

This page offers links to other humor pages, humor information, information on humor research, and more.

http://www.thehumorcollection.org

The Humor Project

The Humor Project was started by Joel Goodman in Sarasota, NY. This Web site offers information about the project, humor discussion boards, materials for purchase, conference information, and more.

http://www.humorproject.com/

The International Society for Humor Studies

The purpose of the International Society for Humor Studies is to encourage and share humor research studies in all areas of academics. This site provides connections to articles, information on conferences, a series of bibliographies, a list of members involved in humor research and humor studies links.

http://www.hnu.edu/ishs/index.htm

The Magic Corner

This site has an online catalog of magic supplies, clowning accessories, and juggling equipment. There is also information about classes and events.

http://www.themagiccorner.com/

World Laughter Tour

This is the official page for the World Laughter Tour. There is information about Laughter Clubs, becoming a certified laughter leader, as well as articles discussing laughter and its contribution to health.

http://www.worldlaughtertour.com

BIBLIOGRAPHY

Abel, M.H. (1998). Interaction of humor and gender in moderating relationships between stress and outcomes. *Journal of Psychology, 132*(3), 267-276. Retrieved July 8, 1998, from http://epnet.com

Adamle, K.N. (2001). *Social interaction in hospice work: A study of humor.* Dissertation, Kent State. Retrieved May 28, 2003, from ProQuest Dissertations.

Adams, P. (2002). Humour and love: The origination of clown therapy. *Postgraduate Medical Journal, 78*(922), 447-478(2). Retrieved October 21, 2003 from Infotrac.galegroup.com

Adams, E.A. & McGuire, F.A. (1986). Is laughter the best medicine? A study of the effects of humor on perceived pain and affect. *Activities, Adaptation and Aging, 8*, 157-175.

Astedt-Kurki, P. & Isola, A. (2001). Humour between nurse and patient, and among staff: Analysis of nurses' diaries. *Journal of Advanced Nursing, 35*(3), 452-458.

Bandura, A. (1997, March). Self-efficacy. *Harvard Mental Health Letter 13*(9). Retrieved August 11, 1997, from http://sbweb2.med.iacnet.com/infotrac/session/362/838/4876526/41xrn_2&bkm_4)A19454921

Barasch, D.S. (1999, March). Sense of humor. *Family Life*, 40-42.

Bariaud, F. (1989). Age differences in children's humor. In P.E. McGhee (Ed.), *Humor and children's development: A guide to practical applications* (pp. 15-45). New York: Haworth Press.

Bartlett, T. (2003). Did you hear the one about the professor? *Chronicle of Higher Education, 49*(46). Retrieved September 22, 2003, from EBSCO Host database.

Bauer, M.E., Gauer, G.J., Luz, C., Silveira, R.O., Nardi, N.B., & von Muhlen, C.A. (1995). Evaluation of immune parameters in depressed patients. *Life Sciences, 57*(7), 655-674.

Baycrest Centre for Geriatric Care. (2003, August 25). *Appreciation of humor doesn't change with age.* Retrieved October 14, 2003, from http://www.baycrest.org/news_2003_baycrest_humoraging.asp

Beck, C.T. (1997). Humor in nursing practice: A phenomenological study. *International Journal of Nursing Studies, 34*(5), 346-352.

Bellert, J. (1989). Humor: A therapeutic approach in oncology nursing. *Cancer Nursing, 12*(2), 65-70.

Bennett, M.P., Zeller, J.M., Rosenberg, L., & McCann, J. (2003). The effect of mirthful laughter on stress and natural killer cell activity. *Alternative Therapies in Health and Medicine, 9*(2), 38-45.

Berger, A.A. (1987). Humor: An introduction. *American Behavioral Scientist, 30*(1), 6-15.

Berk, L.S., Felten, D.L., Tan, S.A., Bittman, B.B., & Westengard, J. (2001). Modulation of neuroimmune parameters during the eustress of humor-associated mirthful laughter. *Alternative Therapies in Health and Medicine, 7*(2), 62-76.

Berk, L.S., Tan, S.A., Fry, W.F., Napier, B.J., Lee, J.W., Hubbard, R.W., et al. (1989, December). Neuroendocrine and stress hormone changes during mirthful laughter. *American Journal of the Medical Sciences, 298*(6), 390-396.

Berk, R.A. (2002). *Humor as an instructional defibrillato: Evidence-based: Techniques in teaching and assessment* . Sterling, VA: Stylus.

Bihn, P. (1995). Starting a humor cart. *Journal of Nursing Jocularity, 5*(2), 32-34.

Bippus, A.M. (2000). Humor usage in comforting episodes: Factors predicting outcomes. *Western Journal of Communication, 64*(4), 359-384.

Boerman-Cornell, W. (2000). "Humor" your students! *Education Digest, 5*(65)56-62. Retrieved July 30, 2003, from EBSCO Host database.

Bokun, B. (1986). *Humour therapy in cancer, psychosomatic diseases, mental disorders, crime, interpersonal and sexual relationships.* London: Vita Books.

Bottari, A.C. (2000). Humor in Healing. *Subconsciously Speaking, 15*(6). Retrieved May 17, 2003, from EBSCO Host database.

Bower, G.H. & Hilgard, E.R. (1981). *Theories of Learning.* Englewood Cliffs, NJ: Prentice-Hall.

Brookfield, S.D. (1986). *Understanding and facilitating adult learning: A comprehensive analysis of principles and effective practices.* San Francisco: Jossey-Bass.

Burger, A.A. (1987). Humor: An introduction. *American Behavioral Scientist, 30*(1), 6-15.

Buxman, K. (1996). 5 rights of humor administration. Presented at the Journal of Nursing Jocularity Humor Skills for the Health Professional Conference, St. Louis, Mo.

Buxman, K. (1998). *Humor as a cost-effective means of stress management.* Retrieved May 9, 2003, from http://www.humorx.com/coststress.html

Buxman, K. (2001). *Mind if I laugh.* Retrieved May 23, 2003, from http://www.humorx.com/mind-laugh.html

Clark, W.N. (2002). What makes babies laugh? *Parenting, 16*(7)191-192. Retrieved May 24, 2003, from EBSCO Host database.

Richard and Hinda Rosenthal Center for Complementary and Alternative Medicine (n.d.). *Clown therapy and the pediatric surgical patient.* Retrieved July 2, 2003, from http://www.rosenthal.hs.columbia.edu/clowntherapy.html

Coffee, G. (1990). *Beyond survival: Building on the hard times—A POW's inspiring story.* New York: Putnam.

Cole, E. (2001). *Humor and grief.* Paper presented at the American Association for Therapeutic Humor Annual Conference, February 2-4, 2001.

Conkell, C., Imwold, C., & Ratliffe, T. (1999). The effects of humor on communicating fitness concepts to high school students. *Physical Educator, 56*(1). Retrieved May 28, 2003, from EBSCO Host database.

Cousins, N. (1979). *Anatomy of an illness as Perceived by the Patient: Reflections on healing and regeration.* New York: Bantam.

Darby, M. (1996). *Humor and the treatment of mental illness: Use it or lose it!* Omaha, NE: Surprise Publishing.

Doskoch, P. (1996). Happily ever laughter. *Psychology Today, 29*(4), 32-36.

Dossey, L. (1996). "Now you are fit to live": Humor and health. *Alternative Therapies in Health and Medicine, 2*(5)8-13. Retrieved May 11, 2003 from EBSCO Host database.

Dowling, J.S. (2002). Humor: A coping strategy for pediatric patients. *Pediatric Nursing, 28*(2), 123-131.

Dworetzky, J.P. & Davis, N.J. (1989). *Human development: A lifespan approach.* St. Paul: West Publishing.

Elderhostel (n.d.). About Elderhostel. Retrieved July 6, 2003 from http://www.elderhostel.org/about/default.asp

Elias, M. (2003). Happy folks live longer than fuddy-duddies. *USA Today.* Retrieved July 1, 2003 from http://www.usatoday.com/news/health/2003093094-happy_x_htm

Ferraro, K.F. (Ed.) (1997). *Gerontology: Perspectives and issues* (2nd ed.). New York: Springer.

Flatter, C. (n.d.). Two to five year olds. In *A look at humor in children through the years* [Electronic version]. Retrieved May 29, 2003, from http://www.sesameworkshop.org/parents/advice/article.php?contentId=738&#2

Fletcher, D. (1991). Editor's note. *Journal of Nursing Jocularity, 1*(4), 3.

Flournoy, E., Turner, G., & Combs, D. (2001). Read the writing on the wall. *Nursing2001, 31*(3), 32cc8-32cc10.

Flowers, J. (2001, May/June). The value of humor in technology education. *The Technology Teacher,* 10-12.

Foltz-Gray, D. (1998). Make 'em laugh: Humor programs can help residents heal—seriously. *Contemporary Longterm Care, 21*(9): 44-46.

Frankl, V.E. (1963). *Man's search for meaning: An introduction to logotherapy.* New York: Simon & Shuster.

Frecknall, P. (1994). Good humor: A qualitative study of the uses of humor in everyday life. *Psychology: A Journal of Human Behavior, 31*(1), 12-21.

Freud, S. (1960). Jokes and their relation to the unconscious. (J. Strachey, Trans.). New York: W.W. Norton. (Original work published 1905).

Fuhr, M. (2002). Coping humor in early adolescence. *Humor, 15*(3), 283-304.

Ford-Martin, P. (2001). Stress. *Gale Encyclopedia of Alternative Medicine.* Retrieved October 1, 2003, from http://www.findarticles.com/P/articles/mi-g2603/is_000 6/ai-26030000686

Gascon, D. (1998). Illness is a laughing matter. *Humor for your health.* Retrieved October 7, 2003, from http://www.humorforyourhealth.com/articles/illness_is_a_laughing_matter.html

Gelkopf, M., Sigal, M., & Kramer, R. (1994). Therapeutic use of humor to improve social support in an institutionalized schizophrenic inpatient community. *The Journal of Social Psychology, 134*(2). Retrieved May 20, 2003, from InfoTrac.

Gibson, L. (1995). Comedy carts, baskets, and humor rooms. In K. Buxman & A. LeMoine (Eds.), *Nursing perspectives on humor.* Staten Island, NY: Power Publications.

Goodboe, M.E. (1995, April). Should security practice andragogy? [Electronic version]. *Security Management, 39*(4). Retrieved July 8, 1997. from http://www.securitymanagement.com

Goodheart, A. (1994). *Laughter therapy: How to laugh about everything in your life that isn't really funny.* Santa Barbara, CA: Less Stress Press.

Goodman, J. (2003). *Making sense of humor.* New Horizons for Learning. Retrieved January 9, 2005 from http://www.newhorizons.org/lifelong/workplace/goodman.htm

Gorfinkle, K.S., Slater, J.A., Bagiella, E., Tager, F.A., & Labinsky, E.B. (n.d.). Clown care and healing. Retrieved July 2, 2003, from The Richard and Hinda Rosenthal Center http://www.rosenthal.hs.columbia.edu/clowncure.html

Groves, D.F. (1991). "A merry heart doeth good like a medicine . . ." *Holistic Nursing Practice, 5*(4), 49-56.

Grow, G. (1996, March 20). *Teaching learners to be self-directed.* Retrieved September 2, 1997, from http://www.longleaf.net/ggrow/SSDL/SSDLIndex.html

Gullickson, C. (1995). Listening beyond the laughter: Communicating through the use of humor. In K. Buxman & A. LeMoine (Eds.), *Nursing perspectives on humor.* Staten Island, NY: Power Publications.

Haig, R.A. (1988). *The anatomy of humor: Biopsychosocial and therapeutic perspectives.* Springfield, IL: Thomas.

Hamilton, R. (2003). *The Joyful Alternative.* Retrieved July 2, 2003, from http://www.rtpnet.org/cahaha/

Harvey, L.C. (1998). *Humor for healing: A therapeutic approach.* San Antonio, TX: Therapy Skill Builders.

PRIMEDIA Intertec. (2001, May). *Have a laugh . . . and maybe alleviate those allergies.* Gale Group. Retrieved October 2, 2003, from http://www.findarticles.com/cf_0/m0FKA/5_63/78476866/p1/article.jhtml?term=laughter

Hayashi, K., Hayashi, T., Iwanaga, S., Kawai, K., Ishii, H., Shoji, S., et al. (2003). Laughter lowered the increase in postprandial blood glucose. *Diabetes Care, 265,* 1651-1652.

Henman, L.D. (2001). Humor as a coping mechanism: Lessons from POWs. *Humor, 14*(1), 83-94.

Hergenhahn, B.R. (1990). *An introduction to theories of personality* (3rd ed.). Englewood Cliffs, NJ: Prentice-Hall.

Herth, K.A. (1995). Humor's role in terminal illness. In K. Buxman & A. LeMoine (Eds.), *Nursing Perspectives on Humor.* Staten Island, NY: Power Publications.

Herzog, J.M. (2004) Birth to two. In *A look at humor in children through the years* [Electronic version]. Retrieved January 9, 2005, from http://www.sesameworkshop.org/parents/advice/article.php?contentId=738&#1

Holland, N.N. (1982). *Laughing: A psychology of humor.* Ithaca, NY: Cornell University Press.

Howe, F.C. (1993). The child in elementary school. *Child Study Journal, 23*(4), 227-372.

Hudson, D. (2001). *Prescription for learning: Humor in the classroom.* Athens State University, Athens, AL. Retrieved March 7, 2004, from http://www.schoolmate.com/news/issues/fall01/fl01chalk.asp

Huitt, W. (2001). Motivation to learn: An overview. *Educational Psychology Interactive.* Valdosta State University. Retrieved April 9, 2005, from http://chiron.valdosta.edu/whuitt/col/motivation/motivate.html

Hunt, A.H. (1993). Humor as a nursing intervention. *Cancer Nursing, 16*(1), 34-39.

Humor in the brain: What happens when we laugh. An interview with Dr. Peter Derks (1995). *Humor & Health Letter, 4*(5).

Humor Matters. (n.d.). Definitions. Retrieved June 25, 2003, from http://www.humormatters.com/definiti.htm

Isen, A.M., Daubman, K.A., & Nowicki, G.P. (1987). Positive affect facilitates creative problem solving. *Journal of Personality and Social Psychology, 52*(6), 1122-1131.

Jancin, B. (2001, March). Laughter benefits heart health, immune system. Retrieved October 15, 2003, from http://www.findarticles.com/p/articles/mi_m0BJI/is_6_31/ai_73181080

Johnson, P. (2002). The use of humor and its influences on spirituality and coping in breast cancer survivors. *Oncology Nursing Forum, 29*(4), 691-695.

Kaplan, R.M. & Pascoe, G.C. (1977). Humorous lectures and humorous examples: Some effects upon comprehension and retention. *Journal of Educational Psychology, 69*(1), 61-65.

Kearsley, G. (1997, March 4). Social Learning Theory. *Exploration in learning & instruction: The theory into practice database.* Retrieved August 9, 1997, from http://tip.psychology.org/

Kelly, L.Y. (1981). *Dimensions of Professional Nursing* (4th ed.). New York: MacMillan.

Kidd, M. (1990, September). Older women learning: Now and always [Electronic version]. *Women's Education-Education des femmes 8.* Retrieved August 29, 1997, from http://www.elibrary.com/

Kiely, K. (2003, March 3). Vietnam POWs forged brotherhood in captivity. *USA Today.* Retrieved June 24, 2003, from http://www.usatoday.come/life/2003-03-pows-usat_x_htm

Kinde, J. (2002). *Being funny on purpose: Developing original humor for your talk.* Retrieved October 3, 2003, from http://www.humorpower.com/original_humor.html

Kingsley, D. (2003, August #29). Jokes not as funny as you get older. Retrieved October 14, 2003, from http://www.abc.net.au/science/news/health/HealthRepublish_932837.htm

Klause, A.C. (1987, February). So what's so funny, anyway? *School Library Journal,* 34-35.

Kleiman, A.M. (1995, April 15). The aging agenda: Redefining library services for a graying population. *Library Journal, 120*(7), 32. Retrieved August 29, 1997, from EBSCO Host databank.

Klein, A. (n.d.). Serious illness is not funny but funny things happen. Retrieved July 2, 2003, from http://www.worldlaughtertour.com/pdfs/Allen_Klein_SERIOUS_ILLNESS_IS_NOT_FUNNY.PDF

Klein, A. (1989). *The healing power of humor.* Los Angeles: J.P. Tarcher.

Klein, A. (1998). *The courage to laugh: Humor, hope, and healing in the face of dying.* New York: J.P. Tarcher/Putnam.

Klein, A. (2001). How can you laugh at a time like this? *Association for Applied and Therapeutic Humor.* Retrieved May 24, 2003, from http://www.aath.org/art_klein01.html

Klein, A.J. (1985). Humor comprehension and humor appreciation of cognitively oriented humor: A study of kindergarten children. *Child Study, 15*(4), 223-234.

Klein, A. (1992, Summer). Storybook humor and early development. *Childhood Education, 68*(4), 213-217.

Knight, B.G. (1996). *Psychotherapy with older adults* (2nd ed.). Thousand Oaks, CA: Sage Publications.

Knowles, M.S. (1978). *The adult learner: A neglected species.* Houston, TX: Gulf.

Kuhn, C. (2003). *The fun factor: Unleashing the power of humor at home and on the job* (2nd ed.). Louisville: Minerva Books.

Kuiper, N.A., Martin, R.A., & Olinger, L.J. (1993). Coping humor, stress, and cognitive appraisals. *Canadian Journal of Behavioral Science, 25*(1), 81-96.

Kutner, L. (n.d.). Insights for parents: Humor as a key to child development. Retrieved May 28, 2003, from http://www.drkutner.com/parenting/articles/humor.html

Labott, S.M. & Martin, R.B. (1987, Winter). The stress-moderating effects of weeping and humor. *Journal of Human Stress, 13*(4), 159-164.

Labott, S.M., Ahleman, S., Wolever, M.E., & Martin, R.B. (1990, Winter). The physiological and psychological effects of the expression and inhibition of emotion. *Behavioral Medicine, 16*(4), 182-189.

Lamp, J.M. (1992). Humor in postpartum education: Depicting a new mother's worst nightmare. *Maternal-Child Nursing, 17*(2), 82-85.

Lawson, W. (2001). Engaging with humour. *Adults Learning, 12*(8). Retrieved July 30, 2003, from EBSCO Host databank.

Lebowitz, K.R. (2002). The effects of humor on cardiopulmonary functioning, psychological well-being, and health status among older adults with chronic obstructive pulmonary disease. (Publication Number: AAT 3049063). Retrieved March 8, 2005, from UMI ProQuest Digital Dissertations.

Lefcourt, H.M. & Martin, R.A. (1986). *Humor and life stress: Antidote to adversity.* New York: Springer-Verlag.

Lefcourt, H.M., Davidson, K., Shepherd, R., Phillips, M., Prakachin, K., & Mills, D. (1995). Perspective-taking humor: Accounting for stress moderation. *Journal of Social and Clinical Psychology, 14*(4), 373-391.

Leigh, E. (2001). *Triumph over tragedy.* Presented at the Association for Applied and Therapeutic Humor, 2001 workshop.

Leise, C.M. (1993). The correlation between humor and the chronic pain of arthritis. *Journal of Holistic Nursing, 11*(1), 82-95. Retrieved December 8, 1998, from EBSCO Host database.

Lippert, L.R. (2001). *Humor exchanges: An ethnographic study of humor as communication between nurses and residents in a long-term care residence* (Publication Number: AAT 3058609). Dissertation retrieved May 28, 2003, from ProQuest Dissertations.

Lomax, R.G. & Moosavi, S.A. (2002). Using humor to teach statistics: Must they be orthogonal? *Understanding Statistics, 1*(2), 113-130.

Long, H.B. (1990). Understanding adult learners. In M.W. Galbraith (Ed.), *Adult learning methods: A guide for effective instruction.* Malabar, FL: R.E. Krieger.

Lumsden, D.B. (1987-88, Winter). How adults learn. *Generations,* pp. 10-15.

Mahony, D.L. (2000). Is laughter the best medicine or any medicine at all? *Eye on Psi Chi, 4*(3), 18-21. Retrieved May 20, 2003, from http://www.psichi.org/pubs/articles/article_81.asp

Mahony, D.L., Burroughs, W.J., & Hieatt, A.C. (2001). The effects of laughter on discomfort thresholds: Does expectation become reality? *Journal of General Psychology, 128*(2), 217-226. Retrieved July 4, 2003, from EBSCO Host database.

Makinen, S., Suominen, T., & Lauri, S. (2000). Self-care in adults with asthma: How they cope. *Journal of Clinical Nursing, 9*(4), 557-565.

Malouf, D. (2003). *How to teach adults in a fun and exciting way* (2nd ed.). Crows Nest, NSW, Australia: Allen & Unwin.

Maranan, J.T. (2001, August). *Laughter may be a better antibiotic: Recent research proves that humor can help you fight germs.* Retrieved October 1, 2003, from http://www.findarticles.com/p/articles/mi_m0NAH/is_6_31/ai_80088276

Martin, R.A. & Lefcourt, H. (1983). Sense of humor as a moderator of the relation between stressors and moods. *Journal of Personality and Social Psychology, 45*(6), 1313-1324.

Martin, R.A. (1989). Humor and the mastery of living: Using humor to cope with the daily stresses of growing up. In P.E. McGhee (Ed.), *Humor and children's development: A guide to practical applications* (pp. 135-154). New York: Haworth Press.

Martin, R.A. (2001). Humor, laughter, and physical health: Methodological issues and research findings. *Psychological Bulletin, 127*(4), 504-519. Retrieved November 27, 2002, from EBSCO Host database.

Masie, E. (2003, March). Make it relevant, interesting . . . and funny. *ITTraining.* Retrieved September 22, 2003, from EBSCO Host database.

McCullough-Brabson, E. (1995, January). Teaching in the Elderhostel program. *Music Educators Journal,* pp. 41-44.

McGhee, P.E. (n.d.). *Humor and health.* Retrieved May 7, 2003, from http://www.holisticonline .com/Humor_Therapy/humor_mcghee_article .htm

McGhee, P.E. (Ed.). (1989). *Humor and children's development: A guide to practical applications.* New York: Haworth Press.

McGhee, P.E. (1994). *How to develop your sense of humor: An 8-step humor development training program for learning to use humor to cope with stress.* Dubuque, IA: Kendall/Hunt Publishing.

McGhee, P.E. (2000). Humor and laughter strengthen your immune system. In P.E. McGhee, *Health, healing and the amuse system: Humor as survival training.* [Electronic Resource]. Retrieved March 9, 2004, from http://www .humor.ch/mcghee/mcghee_00_01.htm

McGhee, P.E. (2001). *Humor your tumor.* Retrieved January 14, 2005, from http://www.laughter remedy.com/humor2.dir/humor5_01.html

Merriam, S.B. & Brockett, R.G. (1997). *The profession and practice of adult education: An introduction.* San Francisco: Jossey-Bass.

Merriam-Webster's new collegiate dictionary (9th ed.). (1985). Springfield, MA: Merriam-Webster.

Minden, P. (2002). Humor as the focal point of treatment for forensic psychiatric patients. *Holistic Nursing Practice, 16*(4), 75-86.

Moore, S. (2002). *Math quiz for emergency department staff.* Retrieved September 3, 2004, from http://www.allnurses.com/

Moran, C.C. (1996). Short-term mood change, perceived funniness, and the effect of humor stimuli. *Behavioral Medicine, 22*(1), 32-38. Retrieved September 19, 1997, from http//www.elibrary. com

Murphy, J.R. (1978). Is it Skinner or nothing? In M. Knowles (Ed.), *Adult learner: A neglected species, Vol. 2.* Houston: Gulf.

Newman, B.M. & Newman, P.R. (1999). *Development through life: A psychological approach (7th ed).* Pacific Grove: Brooks/Cole.

Nezu, A.M., Nezu, C.M., & Blissett, S.E. (1988). Sense of humor as a moderator of the relation between stressful events and psychological distress: A prospective analysis. *Journal of Personality and Social Psychology, 54*(3), 520-525.

Pajares, F. (1997, July 7). Overview of social cognitive theory. Retrieved August 7, 1997, from http://www.emory.edu/EDUCATION/mfp/ eff.html

Pasquali, E.A. (1990). Learning to laugh: Humor as therapy. *Journal of Psychosocial Nursing and Mental Health Services, 28*(3), 31-35.

Pasquali, E.A. (1995). Humor for mentally ill patients. In K. Buxman & A. LeMoine (Eds.), *Nursing perspectives on humor.* Staten Island, NY: Power Publications.

Porterfield, A. (1987). Does sense of humor moderate the impact of life stress on psychological and physical well-being? *Journal of Research in Personality, 21,* 306-317.

Provine, R.R. (2000a). *Laughter: A scientific investigation.* New York: Viking.

Provine, R.R. (2000b). The science of laughter. *Psychology Today, 33*(6), 58-61. Retrieved July 3, 2003, from EBSCO Host database.

Reddy, V., Williams, E., & Vaughan, A. (2002). Sharing laughter: The humour of pre-school children with Down syndrome. *Down's Syndrome Research and Practice, 7*(3), 125-128.

Ritz, S.E. (1995). Survivor humor and disaster nursing. In K. Buxman & A. LeMoine (Eds.), *Nursing perspectives on humor.* Staten Island, NY: Power Publications.

Robinson, D.T. & Smith-Lovin, L. (2001). Getting a laugh: Gender, status, and humor in task discussions. *Social Forces, 80*(1), 123-158.

Robinson, V. (1978) *Humor and the health professions* (1st ed). Thorofare, NJ: Slack.

Robinson, V.M. (1991) *Humor and the health professions* (2nd ed). Thorofare, NJ: Slack.

Rosner, F. (2002). Therapeutic efficacy of laughter in medicine. *Cancer Investigation, 20*(3) 434-436.

Ruch, W., McGhee, P.E., & Hehl, F.J. (1990). Age differences in the enjoyment of incongruity-resolution and nonsense humor during adulthood. *Psychology and Aging, 5*(3), 348-355.

Rx Laughter. (2002). *Laughter tested as pain therapy for children.* Retrieved April 14, 2004, from http://www.rxlaughter.org/pAMA.htm

Salameh, W.A. (1983). Humor in psychotherapy: Past outlooks, present status, and future frontiers. In P.E. McGhee & J.H. Goldstein (Eds.), *Handbook of humor research*: Vol. II (pp. 61-85). New York: Springer-Verlag.

Seaward, B.L. (1992, April). Humor's healing potential. *Health Progress, 73*(3), 66-70.

Schleifer, S.J., Keller, S.E., Bartlett, J.A., Eckholdt, H.M., & Delaney, B.R. (1996). Immunity in young adults with major depressive disorder. *American Journal of Psychiatry, 153*(4), 477-482.

Schrecengost, A. (2001). Do humorous preoperative teaching strategies work? *AORN Journal, 74*(5), 683-689.

Schunk, D.H. (1991). *Learning theories: An educational perspective.* New York: Merrill.

Schwebke, S. (n.d.). *The hospital clown: A closer look.* Retrieved June 30, 2003, from http://www.hospitalclown.com

Schwebke, S. (n.d.). I love you Wollie. *The Hospital Clown Newsletter.* Retrieved March 9, 2004, from http://www.hospitalclown.com/InfoPages/storiesTable.htm

Shade, R. (1991). Verbal humor in gifted students and students in the general population: A comparison of spontaneous mirth and comprehension. *Journal for the Education of the Gifted, 14*(2), 134-150.

Shibles, W. (2002). Humor reference guide: A comprehensive classification and analysis. Retrieved July 5, 2004, from http://facstaff.uww.edu/shiblesw/humorbook/hpreface.html

Socha, T.J. (1994). Children making "fun:" Humorous communication, impression management, and moral development. *Child Study Journal, 24*(3), 237-253.

Smitt, M. (1995, November). *Humor and hospice . . . Not an oxymoron.* Handout from the annual meeting of the American Association of Therapeutic Humor.

Solomon, J.C. (1996, January). Humor and aging well: A laughing matter or a matter of laughing. *American Behavioral Scientist, 39*(3), 249-272.

Strubbe, B. (2003). Getting serious about laughter. *The World and I, 18*(3), 132-140. Retrieved May 29, 2003, from EBSCO Host database.

Struthers, J. (1999). An investigation into community psychiatric nurses' use of humour during client interactions. *Journal of Advanced Nursing, 29*(5), 1197-1204.

Stuart, G.W. & Sundeen, S.J. (Eds.) (1995). *Principles and practice of psychiatric nursing (5th ed.).* St. Louis: Mosby.

Sultanoff, S.M. (1992). *The impact of humor in the counseling relationship.* Originally published in *Laugh it Up,* Retrieved May 29, 2003, from http://www.humormatters.com/articles/therapy2.htm

Sultanoff, S.M. (1994). Choosing the amusing: Assessing the individual's receptivity to therapeutic humor. *Journal of Nursing Jocularity 4*(4), 35-35.

Sultanoff, S.M. (1995). *Levity defies gravity: Using humor in crisis situations.* Retrieved May 24, 2003, from Association for Applied and Therapeutic Humor at http://www.aath.org/art_sultanoff02.html

Sultanoff, S.M. (2000). Using humor for treatment and diagnosis: A shrinking perspective. Originally published in *Therapeutic Humor,* 15(1), 5. Retrieved March 3, 2005, from http://www.humormatters.com/articles/treatmentdiagnosis.htm

Tan, S.A., Tan, L.G., Berk, L.S., Lukman, S.T., & Lukman, L.F. (1997). Mirthful laughter, an effective adjunct in cardiac rehabilitation. *Canadian Journal of Cardiology, 13*(suppl B), 190.

Taylor, I. & Burgess, H. (1995). Orientation to self-directed learning: Paradox or paradigm. *Studies in Higher Education, 20*(1). Retrieved June 3, 1997, from EBSCO Host database.

Tyson, P. (n.d.) Six to eleven. In *A look at humor in children through the years.* Retrieved May 29, 2003, from http://www.sesameworkshop.org/parents/advice/article.php?contentId=738&#3

University of Maryland Medical Center (2005, March 16). *Laughter helps blood vessels function better.* Retrieved April 15, 2005, from www.sciencedaily.com/releases/2005/03/050309111444.htm

Vella, J. (1994). Learning to listen/learning to teach: Training trainers in the principles and practices of popular education. *Convergence, 27*(1). Retrieved June 4, 1997 from http://library.uophx.edu/cgi-bin/prot-bin/main

Wade, S.L., Borawski, E.A., Taylor, H.G., Drotar, D., Yeates, K.O., & Stancin, T. (2001). The relationship of caregiver coping to family outcomes during the initial year following pediatric traumatic injury. *Journal of Consulting and Clinical Psychology, 69*(3), 406-415.

Walsh, T. (n.d.). Funny heart protection: Laughing makes the heart grow stronger. *Healthy Heart Center.* Retrieved May 22, 2004, from http://www.prevention.com/article/0%2C5778%2Cs1-6-75-66-743-1-P%2C00.html

Watkins, A. (1997). Mind-body pathways. In A. Watkins (Ed.), *Mind-Body Medicine.* New York: Churchill Livingstone.

Wells, K. (2001). Humor therapy. In K.M. Krapp & J.L. Longe (Eds.), *The Gale Encyclopedia of Alternative Medicine.* Detroit, MI: Thomson Gale.

Whisonant, R.D. (1998). The effects of humor on cognitive learning in a computer-based environment. Doctorial Dissertation, Virginia Polytechnic Institute. (Publication Number: AAT 9905176). Retrieved March 8, 2005, from UMI ProQuest Digital Dissertations.

Wilson, C.P. (1979). *Jokes: Form, content, use, and function.* New York: Academic Press.

Wiklinski, B.A. (1994). Has humor a meaning for persons adapting to a cancer experience? A phenomenological question (UMI No. 75009). *Dissertation Abstracts International: Section B: The Sciences & Engineering, 54*(12-B).

Wlodkowski, R.J. (1990). Strategies to enhance adult motivation to learn. In M.W. Galbraith (Ed.), *Adult Leaning Methods: A guide for effective instruction.* Malabar, FL: R. E. Krieger.

Wong, P.T. (2003). Humor and laughter in wartime. *International Network on Personal Meaning.* Retrieved June 24, 2003, from http://www.meaning.ca/articles/presidents_column/humor_in_wartime_april03.htm

Wooten, P. (1992). Send in the clowns! Part I. *Journal of Nursing Jocularity, 2*(4), 46-47.

Wooten, P. (1994). *Jest for the health of it!: An interview with William Fry, Jr., MD.* Retrieved August 10, 1998, from http://www.jesthealth.com/frame-articles.html

Wooten, P. (1995). Humor cart for cancer patients: Interview with Terry Bennett. *Journal of Nursing Jocularity, 5*(3), 46-47.

Wooten, P. (1996). Humor: An antidote for stress. *Holistic Nursing Practice, 10*(2), 49-55. Retrieved May 28, 2003, from http://www.jesthealth.com/artantistress9.html

Wooten, P. (1997). *Humor skills for surviving managed care.* Retrieved May 28, 2003, from http://www.jesthealth.com/frame-articles.html

Wooten, P. & Dunkelblau, E. (2001). *Tragedy, laughter, and survival.* Retrieved May 24, 2003, from Association for Applied and Therapeutic Humor at http://www.aath.org/art_woot dunk1.html

World Laughter Tour. (n.d.). *Our History.* Retrieved July 1, 2003, from http://www.worldlaughter tour.com/sections/about/history.asp

Yale–New Haven Children's Hospital (2002). Big Apple Circus Clown Care Unit. Retrieved July 6, 2003, from http://www.ynhh.org/pediatrics/support/clown_care_unit.html

Zemke, R. &. Zemke, S. (1984, March 9). 30 things we know for sure about adult learning. *Innovative Abstracts VI*(8). National Institute for Staff and Organizational Development. Retrieved August 7, 1977, from http://www.hcc.hawaii.edu/education/hcc/fasdev/30things.html

Ziegler, J.B. (1998). Use of humor in medical teaching. *Medical Teacher, 20*(4), 341-348

Ziv, A. (1984). *Personality and sense of humor.* New York: Springer Publishing.

INDEX

PRETEST KEY

Humor in Healthcare:
The Laughter Prescription

1.	b	Chapter 1
2.	d	Chapter 1
3.	c	Chapter 2
4.	a	Chapter 2
5.	d	Chapter 3
6.	d	Chapter 3
7.	b	Chapter 4
8.	d	Chapter 4
9.	b	Chapter 5
10.	a	Chapter 5
11.	c	Chapter 6
12.	c	Chapter 6
13.	d	Chapter 7
14.	a	Chapter 7
15.	a	Chapter 8
16.	b	Chapter 8
17.	c	Chapter 9
18.	b	Chapter 10
19.	b	Chapter 11
20.	a	Chapter 11

Notes

Notes

Notes

Notes

Western Schools® offers over 1,900 hours to suit all your interests – and requirements!

Visit us online at
westernschools.com
for all our latest CE offerings!

REV. 4/16/08